Tenderfoot Teacher

Letters from the Big Bend 1952-1954

D1565448

Tenderfoot Teacher

Letters from the Big Bend 1952-1954

❖ By ❖

AILEEN KILGORE HENDERSON

❖ Foreword by ❖

ROLAND H. WAUER

TCU PRESS · FORT WORTH

Friends of the
Houston Public Library

Copyright ©Aileen Kilgore Henderson 2002
Chisholm Trail Series Number Twenty-One

Library of Congress Cataloging-in-Publication Data

Henderson, Aileen Kilgore, 1921-
Tenderfoot teacher : letters from the Big Bend, 1952-1954 / by Aileen
Kilgore Henderson ; foreword by Roland H. Wauer.
p. cm. -- (The Chisholm Trail series ; no. 21)
Includes bibliographical references.
ISBN 0-87565-264-6 (trade paper : alk. paper)
1. Henderson, Aileen Kilgore, 1921---Correspondence. 2. Big Bend
National Park (Tex.)--Description and travel. 3. Natural
history--Texas--Big Bend National Park. 4. Big Bend National Park
(Tex.)--Biography. 5. Teachers--Texas--Big Bend National
Park--Correspondence. 6. Henderson, Aileen Kilgore, 1921---Homes and
haunts--Texas--Big Bend National Park. I. Title. II. Series.
F392.B53 H37 2002
976.4'932--dc21
                              2002000555

Cover and text design by Bill Maize; Duo Design Group

(Photo opposite)
Panther Junction School, with the Chisos Mountains in the background.

❖

To all of those
who welcomed me into their lives
And helped me learn to love
the Big Bend.

❖

CHISHOLM TRAIL SERIES

Number Twenty-one

❖ CONTENTS ❖

When I was asked to write a foreword to Aileen Henderson's book, *Tenderfoot Teacher: Letters from the Big Bend, 1952-1954*, I was at first skeptical. I had read many other manuscripts and publications about the early days in Big Bend, and I assumed that Aileen's manuscript would be little more than a rehashing of various events within the park during its early years. After all, what could a teacher who had spent only two years in the park add to the tremendous amount of literature that might be of interest to me and the host of other Big Bend advocates?

However, on reading the manuscript, I discovered that it was full of fascinating details about a different time in the park's history and written from a very different perspective from any of the other authors I had read. That made it most worthwhile. It provided details about one person's experience in the Big Bend Country that needed to be published. So I agreed to write this foreword, and I have gone about it with considerable enthusiasm.

I discovered in reading Aileen's letters that she had taken the teaching job at Panther Junction, the park headquarters, with considerable hesitancy. She wrote that Big Bend was so isolated that she doubted her senses for going to such a place. Her initial reaction to Big Bend Park, at the end of a seventy-mile drive from the nearest town of any size, Marathon, is not unusual for many folks who see the region for the first time. And she was "quaking" in her boots on her first meeting with the president of the school board. But she immediately liked him and all the other members of the board. She became not only the schoolteacher for grades four through seven but also the school principal. Another teacher—Gertrude—taught the lower grades. And on further reading it was obvious that in only a few days she began to appreciate the magnificent scenery: "I've become reconciled to the mountains. They look more beautiful each day." And in a letter a year later she wrote: "The scenery here is so beautiful it's a pity to stay indoors. I'm still in awe of it all." Her about-face is also typical.

Aileen had written about a time twelve years prior to the period that I worked in the park (1966-1972). But I found that she mentioned a number of folks that I either knew personally or had heard about. Those individuals helped me put her park years into perspective. For instance, the Dotts—Boots, Nealie, and the three boys—had been good friends of mine when I worked at Death Valley National Park (Monument at the time). I found her descriptions of these folks fascinating: they were the same wonderful people that I had known in an earlier time. Other mutual friends included Pete Koch, a local photographer; Mac Waters, one of the park's maintenance personnel still present during my tenure; and Pat Miller, a good friend with whom I later worked at Great Smoky Mountains National Park.

Aileen's letters tell about being befriended by numerous park neighbors during her residency there. I had the same experience, for people in the parks are like an extended family. Even the grocer, Willie, who delivered her weekly groceries from Marathon, was a member of that support group. She mailed her orders in on Wednesdays, and Willie delivered the groceries on Sunday mornings. If his customer was not at home, he simply entered the house and put the groceries away. Her description of the folks living at Panther Junction and their activities brought back many good memories of the experiences my family and I had during our stay in the park.

Aileen also wrote about the various social aspects of the park. She apparently was a well-liked individual, by both the Park Service adults and children. She was even invited to a meeting of the "Panther Club, the boy's club here." The boy's took her "up the mountain to their Panther Club camp. Later one mother laughed and said that the boys really were honoring the teacher as no other female had gotten to see their camping place."

Her letters were filled with dinner invitations to various homes and to numerous picnics at scattered sites throughout the park. These picnics were held at such lovely places as Oak Creek, below the Window, Dugout, the oasis along the road to Boquillas, and on the Lost Mine Trail. And there were many times when several families got together for a dance or party. Her description of a chivaree for a newly married couple was one good example: "Later we all went up to the Basin to join everyone who lives there for an event they call a chivaree— what's done to newly married couples to torture them. Late at night we surrounded Bertyl and Jack Lewis' house with every kind of noisemaker possible, awakening them with a terrible din. We made them come outside, tousled and sleepy, in the chill night and ride burros! Then everybody danced past 2:00 A.M.!"

Many of the meals involved food that undoubtedly became favorites. Anyone reading about some of those dishes—"son-of-a-gun-stew," a "luscious chocolate cake made with Irish potatoes," "chicken and mushroom sauce served over waffles," and raisin-and-nut coffeecake—cannot help but have their taste buds awakened.

Aileen also mentioned various organized activities. These ranged from canasta parties at the K-Bar to a party to honor George Washington, to Spanish lessons and ceramics classes. She attended receptions for newlyweds and new arrivals and farewell parties for families being transferred and described the arrival of the new park superintendent and his family: "Mary gave a reception in honor of the new superintendent and his family, the Garrisons. It was a lively affair. Everybody in the park came, and some people from ranches outside and even some from Alpine. I poured coffee, if you can imagine that, me sitting at a lace-covered table pouring coffee from a silver coffee pot."

Farewell parties were often rather sad affairs, for people of whom one had grown quite fond were moving on to a new assignment. The departures of the Gibbs, the Sholleys, and the Dotts, all close friends, left Aileen with sadness but wonderful memories. Such is a nature of the Park Service. Those being transferred are eager to experience new and wonderful places, make new friends, and also to see some that they had known in previous assignments, while those left behind are expected to continue with their daily activities.

Aileen also wrote about places in the park that were undoubtedly her favorites, and many of those sites continue to be popular places to visit even today. Some mutual favorites included Dagger Flat, The Window, Lost Mine Trail, Oak Creek, Santa Elena Canyon, and Hot Springs. She made many trips to Hot Springs, where Etta Koch operated a store. Aileen's descriptions covered a period before the store was closed; the Park Service later restored the building as one of the park's major historical sites.

A book titled *Big Bend, A Homesteader's Story* describes J. O. Langford's efforts to establish a business at that same remote site at the mouth of Tornillo Creek, while trying to recover his health. Langford described his experiences during the first decade of the twentieth century. And Etta Koch recently (1999) published some of her Big Bend reminiscences in a personalized account titled "Lizards on the Mantel, Burros at the Door." Etta discussed her contacts with Maggie Smith, who operated the Hot Springs store just prior to

Etta's involvement. She described Maggie as someone with unlimited energy and a "sense of humor and kindly interest in people which drew them into the store in spite of themselves." According to Aileen, some folks called Maggie a "river renegade. Some say she smuggles illegal materials (I don't know what) into this country, but she is an angel to the poor Mexicans down there, they say." John Jameson (1996) later pointed out that Maggie was "called by many the 'godmother to the Mexican people.'"

Aileen often visited Dagger Flat. This large area along the western slope of Dagger Mountain contains thousands of giant dagger yuccas, and during late March, when hundreds can come into bloom at the same time, it is a magical place. In fact, *Plants of Big Bend National Park*, a marvelous, comprehensive book by W. B. McDougall and Omer E. Sperry, uses an illustration of flowering giant daggers on its cover. I assume that Aileen obtained a copy of this book, which was published in 1951 and has since become a classic.

The McDougall-Sperry book was one of the very few Big Bend books available during Aileen's residence in the mid-1950s. There were, however, a number of technical reports on the park resources that were written by various scientists who surveyed the area prior to park establishment. A host of Big Bend books appeared not long afterwards, as more and more people became enamored with that part of the state.

Two books appeared during the 1950s, soon after Aileen's time: *The Big Bend Country of Texas*, by Virginia Madison, and *The Way I Heard It*, by Walter Fulcher. Both include stories, some true, some not so true, about the Big Bend region. The Madison book is especially worthwhile because it contains information on a wide variety of topics ranging from people to cattle to mining to the making of the park.

One of my longtime favorite books is no longer in print. It is Carlysle Graham Raht's *The Romance of Davis Mountains and Big Bend Country*. This book was privately published by the Rahtbooks Company in 1963 and covers the greater Big Bend country. The discussion of Indian raids and the Comanche Trail cannot be equaled.

Ross Maxwell, a geologist and the park's first superintendent, wrote another of the early publications—*The Big Bend of the Rio Grande*. Although the Maxwell book is principally about the fascinating geology of the region, it also includes a good smorgasbord of historic facts. And even though this book first appeared in 1968, it is still available. A second Maxwell book, simply titled *Big Bend Country*, appeared in 1985. This book deals principally with the history of the park.

At least two other publications cover the park's history, including the establishment of the park itself: Ronnie Tyler's very creditable *The Big Bend: A History of the Last Texas Frontier*, published by the National Park Service in 1975, and John Jameson's *The Story of Big Bend National Park*, published in 1996. These authors take a slightly different approach to the history of the region and park, and both books are well worth reading.

Clifford B. Casey, a longtime history professor at Alpine's Sul Ross State University, produced a series of reports and papers on the Big Bend Country. Several of those reports, commissioned by the National Park Service, were published in 1969 by the National Park Service Division of History in a paperback book titled *Soldiers, Ranchers and Miners in the Big Bend*. And in 1972, a second more general history book, sponsored by the Brewster County Historical Survey Committee, appeared: *Mirages, Mysteries and Reality: Brewster County, Texas, The Big Bend of the Rio Grande*. Topics covered in Casey's first book are clear from the title, and his 1972 book covers an amazing assortment of history of the greater Big Bend region.

Two additional books on Big Bend "tales" were written by Elton Miles: *Tales of The Big Bend* was published in 1976, and a follow-up book, *Stray Tales of the Big Bend*, appeared much later in 1993. These two books include stories about a wide assortment of topics, ranging from religion to water witching, "Chisos Ghosts," Fort Leaton, Terlingua, San Vicente, and Glenn Springs.

There were no publications available on the natural history of the Big Bend area, except for the McDougall-Sperry book, until my two books. *Birds of Big Bend National Park and Vicinity*, was published by the University of Texas Press in 1972; it has been revised twice. The most recent version—*A Field Guide to the Birds of the Big Bend*—appeared in 1996. And *Naturalist's Big Bend*, the first and only comprehensive natural history publication, appeared one year later. This book was completely updated and released as a two-author publication in 2001 by Texas A&M University Press. In 1997, *For All Seasons: A Big Bend Journal*, a compendium of my notes over a thirty-five-year period in the park, was published. And finally, *Butterflies of West Texas Parks and Preserves* appeared in 2001.

Aileen also wrote about the various wild animals found in the park. She fed skunks, coyotes, foxes, and javelinas at her front door. Her October 27, 1952, letter describes her efforts to save a baby skunk from "a monstrous owl taller than my knees clutching my small skunk that had squirted all over the porch." She continued: "I laid it on the patio under a box fixed so that if it came to it could get out but the owl couldn't get in. I crawled back in bed but my house was so odorized I couldn't sleep. It got worse, I couldn't breathe. I shut the windows, opened the air wick and set it on the floor right under my nose but it did no good." The odor stayed with her for several days until she was forced to discard her shoes—she had walked in the spray that night while trying to save her baby skunk.

She also wrote about a favorite fox that she fed at her front door every night. On December 1, 1953, she wrote: "At three o'clock one morning I heard a great noise on my patio. When I turned the light on there was a fox wrestling with a milk bottle. I had forgotten to put food out so I guess he was tired of waiting."

On hikes she was constantly on the lookout for a mountain lion. Although other folks in the park saw these large predators on rare occasions, it wasn't until her second year—on March 10—that she finally saw her first panther. That evening she began her letter to Art, the friend she eventually married, with the following: "I saw a panther—I saw a panther!! Just now coming through Green Gulch! We had been talking about lions, and suddenly this one appeared on the left of the road, only a few feet from us." That incident seemed like a fitting finale to her many adventures. At the end of the 1954 school year she left the park and in December 1954 married Park Ranger Art Henderson.

ROLAND H. WAUER
AUGUST 2001

The Last Frontier: Letters from the Big Bend Region of Texas 1952–1954

In January 1952 I was teaching forty-three fourth graders at a public school in Northport, Alabama, for $1700 per year. Every minute of my spare time was taken up with lesson preparations, in-service meetings, countywide meetings, home visitations, and special projects. My life seemed really grim that winter, and I resolved to make a change.

I remembered that during WWII, when I served in the Women's Army Corps in Texas, I had heard talk about a wild and beautiful area of the state called the Big Bend. It was a place where a Texas Ranger dared not go alone, where panthers roamed free, where lost treasure waited to be found, where ghosts haunted the Chisos Mountains. Within the Big Bend National Park, the Rio Grande wound through three spectacular canyons.

I thought, "Why not go there to teach? Not to the Big Bend itself—they wouldn't have schools there—but to the nearest town." Looking at the map, I found Alpine which appeared to be about one hundred miles from the Big Bend. I wrote a letter to the Alpine Board of Education, applying to teach in their school.

The Alabama winter turned to spring, the spring was ready to become summer, but no reply came. Despite the silence, I resigned from the Northport school without any idea of what I would do. Just before the last day of school a letter arrived, not from Alpine, but from a place called Panther Junction in the Big Bend itself! From the president of the Panther Junction School board, the letter said that the Alpine superintendent of schools had given them my name. They were looking for an outside teacher with a degree in education for their new school. They especially wanted someone who could teach science, a subject their students had never studied. They offered me the fabulous salary of $2600 a year! I accepted without a second thought.

That summer my sister Francys, who lived in San Diego, came home for a visit. I arranged to drive back to San Diego with her and her dog Bridget in August, stopping off at Big Bend National Park as we went west to see the school and meet the school board.

I was not prepared for what I found—the wildness, the limitless space, the isolation, and the exuberant Texas children. It was true the school was new, but far from finished. It sat alone, surrounded by arroyos and backed up against barren mountains. Eventually there would be an apartment attached to it for me to live in. Rocks, rocks, piled everywhere, and the desert heat was scorching.

After two days, I went on to San Diego for several weeks of sightseeing and enjoyment of the ocean, museums, historical sites, theaters, restaurants, and begonia gardens. It was wonderful, and the San Diego City School System had a teacher shortage! I came very close to staying there, but I had signed a contract. I felt honor bound to fulfill it. I boarded the train in California and headed for Marathon, Texas, with a heavy and fearful heart.

During the next two years I wrote letters to Alabama: to my father working for the Frisco Railroad at Boligee; my mother and sister Mary Alice living at our home in Brookwood; my sister Jane living in Tuscaloosa; and to my sister Francys in San Diego, California. Later I wrote letters to a ranger, Arthur A. Henderson, whom I met at Panther Junction in April of 1953. Those edited letters make up this book.

❖ PART ONE ❖

A Greenhorn in Wild Country
August 1952 — July 1953

Dear Daddy,

Yesterday Francys and I ate lunch at Marathon, just before turning off on the nearly seventy-mile stretch to Big Bend. Three or four boys were in the cafe eating. They were in constant motion, cuffing and knocking each other between bites of food, hitting so hard they would nearly fall off the stools. Back in the kitchen I saw two other boys struggling each other around amongst the pots and pans. If this was a sample of Big Bend youth, I was ready to pass by and not come back.

I guess I was looking for boogers anyway. As we sped through the park we stopped to let Bridget out of the car to relieve herself. The ground was solid rock and so hot the poor dog couldn't stand still on it. I was stepping out one door with her while Francys was stepping out on the driver's side when I heard a sinister hissing noise. "Rattlesnake!" I thought and almost broke my leg getting back in the vehicle and trying to save Bridget. Francys checked the tires for escaping air, but they were all right. The noise swelled louder and closer. We discovered a big whirlwind approaching us, then retreating, coming near, then drawing away. After that we found that there's always at least one big whirlwind in sight, and once from atop a middle-sized mountain we saw four huge ones! We decided we'd better drive slowly in order to dodge the whirlwinds, unsure of what they might do to the car. Enduring all those hot miles through those parched mountains just about wrecked me by the time we arrived at a settlement, which turned out to be Panther Junction, at 3:00 P.M.

We left the main road, driving past five houses, a teeny-weeny gray building that some men were working on (an outhouse was in its yard) to a new-looking headquarters building. My courage failed me. I could not go inside and introduce myself as the new teacher. I told Francys to speed, speed, and let's escape. So we climbed ten miles farther over two or three mountains, past barrels of water (in case the car overheated), till at last we came to the Basin where the tourist cabins are. Our cabin turned out to be attractive with many windows, comfortable beds, and a kerosene lamp. We noticed a free lecture about the park was scheduled that night, and we should have gone but I wasn't able.

The altitude was 5400 feet—I couldn't hear, my head ached, and I kept thinking about having to reveal my identity next day. In the morning I stayed in bed as long as I could, lingered at breakfast as long as I could, and dawdled in the bathroom, but finally at ten o'clock I had to go to the motel office and inquire about the man I was to see.

The motel clerk told me I'd find him back at the headquarters where we had been the afternoon before, so down through the rough, wild mountains we drove and into Panther Junction again. I entered the headquarters quaking in my boots. The man I needed to see was there and turned out to be very nice. He took Francys and me to the school (which was the unfinished building we had noticed) but it looked larger now that we were closer to it—it was not so dwarfed by the mountains and the desert surrounding it. And that was no outhouse in its yard, at least not for the teacher. There will be two schoolrooms with one wall all windows looking out over a beautiful valley. I will have hot water, a bathroom, gas cooking stove, electric refrigerator, sink, and a furnished bedroom heated by a furnace, but I have to pay $30 a month rent. I didn't expect that.

Everybody was very cordial. We lunched at the home of board member Bob Gibbs, assistant superintendent of the park. His wife, Mary, served a main dish she called chicketti, and it was delicious. She gave us the recipe. Mary made a point of taking me over to the superintendent's house to meet his wife who opened the door only a few inches, did not invite us in, and was not really welcoming. But Mary was gracious enough for the two of them.

While we were in the park I met several of the students who seemed civilized enough, and I attended a meeting of the board of trustees at 1:00 P.M. where I met Gertrude, the other teacher. The board had us choose the furniture for our schoolrooms, and they told us they're ordering new teachers' desks and green blackboards with yellow chalk to use on them.

I don't know if I'll ever get used to the mountains, but if I do I should enjoy the place. If one of our Alabama calves were in Big Bend, though, he couldn't find enough bushes to keep him alive for one day, I'm afraid.   AK

SEPTEMBER 11, 1952

THURSDAY NIGHT - PANTHER JUNCTION, BIG BEND NATIONAL PARK, TEXAS

Dear Francys,

I have a letter half-written to you but it is so garbled I'm going to start over. I started it yesterday and went to sleep over it late last night, so it doesn't make sense. I'm having a wonderful time; I've become reconciled to the mountains. They look more beautiful each day. When the folks point out Alsate, the Apache chief who haunts the Chisos, or saddles or lions chasing mice, I examine all the peaks in sight, and sometimes I can even locate the figure they are talking about.

But let me tell you what's happened to me since I left you in California. In El Paso we were delayed two-and-a-half hours, causing us to arrive in Marathon at 6:00 A.M. All that night I hadn't slept a wink. When I crept off the train, the only passenger for Marathon, nobody was stirring except a fellow loading freight. I guess he could see I was frozen from fright and the train's air-conditioning so he invited me into the office where it was considerably warmer. He told me I could go out to the park with the postman. After we chatted a while he invited me to go across the ditch with him—he called it an arroyo—for a cup of coffee. Afterwards, his promise to see that the postman didn't leave for the park without me left me free to go to the grocery store he told me about.

The grocer, Willie, was very helpful too. He said the bus runs from Marathon to the park only on Friday—one trip a week. While I shopped, Willie stationed his hired help at the store door to watch the post office so the postman wouldn't escape. Then he put my groceries in a box and sent it over to the post office. When I returned to the depot the young man there had already sent my baggage to the post office too so I was ready to go.

At nine o'clock I squeezed into a loaded-down vehicle with the postman, his wife, and their little bug-eyed dog. As we sped along I could look at the scenery more calmly than when I came with you—I was not so horrified. At the first ranger station, Persimmon Gap, we met Mr. Sholly, the chief ranger and president of the school board. He had not received my letter saying I was coming. He said the school wasn't finished because of trouble getting plumbers and electricians, but that I should go to his house at Panther Junction and make myself at home.

And so I did. Mrs. Sholly is attractive and kind. She is seeing that I meet as many parents and children as possible before school begins Monday the 15th. Last night I had a delicious supper with the Gibbs family in their back-yard and watched a lovely sunset. We could see a striped mountain range over in Mexico that changed to all colors and shades as darkness came.

Johnny Gibbs feeding a skunk.

When I returned to the Shollys' they were sitting in their yard, which has a stone wall around it. The night was dark and cool. As we sat talking a beautiful mid-size skunk squeezed under the gate and strolled around our feet and under the table, searching for crumbs. Soon a small skunk came under the gate, and Danny Sholly handed it a piece of bread. Then the queen of them all appeared—a broad, plump skunk that had such a wide white stripe down her back I couldn't see her black sides. She confronted the small skunk and snatched its bread. The small one backed away, dancing and fussing like an angry squirrel. We gave them more bread. They were still in the yard when we went in to bed.

Tonight after supper (we had fried dove) the three came back again. They nosed around our feet intent on finding food and paying no attention to us. Danny collected the dove bones and piled them on a box. The skunks chewed the bones like cats and then came prying about our feet searching for more. They looked so silky I could hardly resist touching one, but George Sholly said that would be dangerous.

This afternoon I went panther hunting with Danny, Betsy Koch, and a man named Joe from Los Angeles who is visiting at Panther Junction. We started out where the Lost Mine Peak sign is in the Basin and climbed part way up Casa Grande to a spring where mountain lions are supposed to lurk. We saw about ten beautiful deer at various times, some with antlers, some without.

I may sound unkind, but I laughed so hard at Joe I nearly fell off the mountain. He is decrepit, can't hear well, and is highly excitable. He was wearing what looked like a British admiral's hat this afternoon and carrying two cameras plus a lighted cigarette. Whenever Betsy, Danny, or I spotted a deer we'd pull his shirt to get his attention. Then he'd stumble around amongst the rocks trying to find the animals in his camera sights. Sometimes, when each of us sighted deer in different places at the same time, he was lunging every which way.

We rested at the spring, then started down the sharp steep trail. Joe went first, and it was as if he stepped on a down escalator—the rocks rolled under him like wheels. He sped away down the mountain, standing on his feet but completely out of control, bumping into trees, boulders, and century plants. From up by the spring I watched wondering how it could end. Betsy and

Danny, lower down, stood paralyzed. Finally Joe's feet shot out from under him, and he continued down the mountain on his sit-upon, clutching at the bushes he passed in a cloud of dust. Half the rocks on the mountain rolled with him. I controlled myself as long as I could, but as I groped my way down the trail on all fours, I laughed in a most shameful way.

When the three of us reached Joe, he had picked himself up, collected his cameras, straightened his hat, and lit a new cigarette. We finished the descent with more dignity, still peering right and left for lions. Not a one did we see, but plenty of deer were in evidence.

Joe took us over to concessions and bought us Cokes before we started our return trip to Panther Junction. Joe drives a car the same way he descends mountains—out of control and very fast. As we whizzed along the road, three deer walked in front of the car and stopped to look at us approaching them. Joe was like an octopus as he grabbed for his cigarette, the two cameras, the brakes, and his admiral's hat all at the same time. He leaped out of the car while it was still rolling and tried with first one and then the other camera to make a picture. In his excitement he never could see the deer in the viewfinder. Before we reached Panther Junction we stopped once more, and he did succeed in making a picture of two deer grazing. AK

SEPTEMBER 13, 1952 - THURSDAY

Dear Mama,

I'm safely here in Big Bend, and everything looks fine. The school is going to be marvelous—everything the best. For my apartment the school board bought a set of dishes modeled after Russell Wright's, a set of silver plate, and a platform rocker. The bed has an innerspring mattress and a bolster to dress it up as a sofa in the daytime. I'm pleased with all of it. I will probably move in on Sunday.

School starts Monday. I'm the principal as well as a classroom teacher—imagine that. I hope there's not so much work I can't enjoy life here. Fourth through seventh grades will be mine, first through third the other teacher's.

Last night was the meeting of the Panther Club, the boys' club here. They have a camping place up on the mountain where they keep a cupboard of food.

The first day I was here four of the boys took me walking to the schoolhouse, the windmill that pumps the water for this settlement, and then up the mountain to see their Panther Club camp. Later one mother laughed and said the boys really were honoring the teacher as no other female had gotten to see their camping place. AK

SEPTEMBER 14, 1952

Dear Mama,

I haven't gotten any mail since I've been here though I've heard that I have mail over at the Basin, ten miles from here. I feel like I'm on another planet, being so out of touch—no newspapers or magazines. And I'll be so glad to be settled by myself, alone, with my things unpacked. All the people have been hospitable, but I know it is taxing for them to have the schoolteacher staying in their homes, and I long to get my shoes under a bed I can call my own.

Friday night the community had a get-together where I met the remainder of my children and parents. I am going to have two cute Mexican children. One of them has a tongue-twister name, spelled Eligio but pronounced El-lee´he ul.

Yesterday most of the community worked on the school and my quarters. It's all going to be handsome and comfortable. My kitchen unit is special. I can't wait to unpack my recipes and start cooking. I hope I have the time . . . sigh. The climate is wonderful, and these mountains are fascinating to watch after the first shock passes. The nights are especially beautiful and cool. Living at Panther Junction is different from being shut in by the mountains in the Basin. Here I can breathe.

I don't know yet if I'll be allowed a Christmas vacation. The trustees had planned to make up the time we've lost (two weeks) during the holidays, but I protested so violently that they looked taken aback and now are thinking the matter over.

Today some of the community is at the school working again. This afternoon the books from the old school will be brought over from the Basin, and in the morning the new school year will open at eight o'clock. We will leave after a few preliminaries. But starting next day we will go to school from eight till three with one hour out for lunch.

The wild life is the most interesting thing of all here. Last night we looked out on the Gibbs' front lawn to see a big buck deer with a fine head of antlers. He was drinking from the water pan. The skunks came around as usual—the fat, beautiful mother skunk, the child skunk, and the papa skunk. Beautiful quail come in the yards to drink, and I've seen several rabbits. I can hardly wait until I get in my own place so I can fix watering troughs and food to lure them.

For breakfast this morning Mary Gibbs served a raisin-and-nut coffeecake, fried eggs with Mexican sauce, orange juice, and coffee. I stayed at the assistant superintendent's house last night because the Shollys, with whom I've been staying, had three guests from Marathon. George Sholly is the chief park ranger.

On Friday night all the park personnel met at the recreation hall, and a man named Joe who is visiting in the park put on a show. Joe has been in *Ripley's Believe-it-or-Not* and has appeared on television programs. He took three of us on a lion-hunting expedition one day, and he is very funny. At Joe's show I met the rest of my children and their parents. We will have two brothers, one fourteen and the other sixteen, from a ranch outside the park. They'll be in first grade because they've never had a chance to go to school before. They are shy but seem like nice boys.

Don't be worried if you do not hear from me for a while. I'm going to be struggling to settle into school and my apartment. I feel right sorry for myself, sigh—and mail goes out only three times a week, too. AK

SEPTEMBER 14, 1952

Dear Daddy,

Tomorrow is the day—school begins! Woe is me! But I'll be glad to get the business started so I can judge how things are going to be. The school is certainly handsome and modern, and the trustees have provided everything for my comfort in the apartment.

The climate here is most enjoyable—a breeze blows in the daytime, and the nights are cool and beautiful. The people sit in their yards and watch the animals stroll about even with the porch lights on. At night the park belongs to the animals and they know it. I hope to lure some of them to my yard when I'm moved in. Maybe I can move tomorrow, as school will not last very long. You should see my kitchen unit—a little four-burner stove, sink, and refrigerator with cabinets above it. The unit cost between $500 and $600. AK

SEPTEMBER 21, 1952

Dear Daddy,

I was up at six-thirty this Sunday morning, cooked my breakfast, and studied my Sunday-school lesson for this day. There is no church nearer than Marathon, eighty miles away, but the children have Sunday school in the Basin, ten miles farther into the mountains. I plan to go sometime, but they have canceled it for today as all the children are going to Alpine to the circus.

I appreciate the clippings you all send to keep me posted on events. I don't see a newspaper but the families here pass around their magazines. I received my first batch yesterday.

My trunk arrived Friday, the 19th. How much did it cost? I see on the card that it weighed 158 pounds. How in the world did you all manage it? AK

SEPTEMBER 21, 1952

Dear Everybody,

I did not move into my apartment until Friday afternoon. For my first three days here I stayed at the Sholly home. He is chief ranger for the park. For the rest of the time I stayed at the Gibbs' home. He is assistant superintendent of the park, but he carries on most of the superintendent's work as the superintendent doesn't seem to be functioning. I have not met him so I don't know the story on him.

The Shollys and the Gibbs have tended to my every want and luxury and have carried me to all the social affairs. Mary Gibbs was a dietitian (she is Christian Scientist) before she married, and the meals at her house were always superb. One night when her husband was away camping she made a chicken-and-mushroom sauce to serve over waffles and also a syrup and butter mixture to turn the waffles into a dessert. Delicious! Mary has provided me with two rugs, a lamp, towel racks, dishtowels, hangers, cookies—she even froze a bowl of the delicious chicken-and-pimento dish I enjoyed so much (the chicketti I mentioned before) for me to have on hand. She has helped with my grocery list and provided potted plants for the school. Reece Sholly has helped me a great deal too, and I could not wish for things to be any different.

I enjoy my house, and I like living alone. The school sits on a rise, and wherever I look I see a beautiful view. The climate is wonderful; cool, plenty of sunshine, lovely clouds in the afternoon, clear sky always at night. The climate is dry, but I feel well and energetic.

No animals seem to come around my house. This morning I put out water and bread for the birds; I hope to get a bigger water container (my present one is a hub cap I found in the trash bin) and lure the larger animals. I am in love with the skunks and the deer. Buck deer, five and six in a group, come to the Gibbs' to drink from their water bowl, and a mama coyote and her baby come there nearly every day.

Yesterday was a very social day for me—the first day in my house. I was up at 6:30 to see the sun rise over the mountains, but before I finished washing dishes and converting my bed into the daytime sofa, four little boys had accumulated, one by one. We entertained each other while I went on with my work. More little boys gathered as some of the fathers came to paint on the school.

Everybody around here dotes on coffee, so the boys and I served the men coffee for mid-morning, and we had orange juice Mary Gibbs had put in my refrigerator. When I was ready to be alone I sent the boys away to play. But in the afternoon Bruce, the superintendent's son, came back. He was called home soon (just across the ravine, or as they say here the arroyo), but before long he was back to stay until I went to borrow the Gibbs' ironing board at five o'clock. I didn't mind, as I was sewing, and he is so interested in learning things. He is a third grader, in the other teacher's room. He's already asked me if I am coming back next year so he can be in my room. That's because I am teaching science, which is what interests him most. None of the children here have ever had science of any kind, so they are having a fine time with this universe unit I am teaching. We don't have the partition between the rooms yet, but we should get it next week. However, the two rooms don't bother each other at all.

I have only seven (yes, seven!) students—one in fourth, two in fifth, three in sixth, and one in the seventh. I am supposed to get one more fourth and one more sixth—the Mexican brother and sister. They are delayed coming because their father participated in a knife fight in Terlingua (on the border) and the whole family is with him in Alpine where he is hospitalized.

So far school has been all pleasure. My children are likable, and the other teacher is, too. The children have never before played games with their teacher supervising, and they are enjoying play period too. All of them are good readers and seem well grounded in the skills of reading, 'riting and 'rithmetic, but they've not had any fun in school before.

The climax to yesterday was last night. I really need a whole letter to tell about that one event. The Gibbs family took me many miles down to Hot Springs, on the Rio Grande and the border, to a barbecue. I wore the sheer purple dress Francys made for me with the tiered skirt, a wide red belt with gold buckle, and red shoes! Maggie Smith, an older woman who lives there, is what people call a character, a "river renegade." Some say she smuggles illegal materials (I don't know what) into this country, but she is an angel to the poor Mexicans down there, "they" say. The park people tell me the *Saturday Evening Post* published an article about Mrs. Smith and Hot Springs a while back. Every two years she gives a barbecue for the entire countryside, and this happened to be the year and the day for it. The road down to Hot Springs is so narrow it is one way. Another one-way road brings you back. We lost considerable altitude going there. Mr. Gibbs told me I would see the West much as it was during frontier days, so I was prepared not to miss a thing.

Hot Springs is beautiful in a different way from Panther Junction. Less color but strange formations of hills and rocks. From the house where the barbecue was held we walked a short way to the river, which is low now, and on the dry part of the riverbed I found a rock that I am adding to my rock box.

There was a large crowd, not only from the park but from nearby ranches. I am amazed at the number of eligible men around, and most of them seem quite acceptable. One that I met last night was tall and lean, with cowboy legs. He runs a farm down on the river.

A Mexican man was in charge of the barbecue pit that was a deep round hole like a well. The meat (a whole calf and a whole goat) had been wrapped several times in wet cloth, then in wet tow sacks, and lowered into the pit some time yesterday. It was cooked long and slow over red-hot coals. When the barbecue was ready, bringing it up out of the hole and ripping the coverings off of each large piece was quite a ceremony. The meat was so tender it fell off the bones as the cooks laid it in the pans.

Three men stood by iced tubs handing out drinks—any kind of soft drink and beer. Mrs. Smith's house had a wide front gallery nearly as long as a football field, because she has rooms for tourists. Her decorations were tall canes with fuzzy, cat-tailish tops from the river, tied in shocks like corn. I noticed the roof of the porch and the sunshield on the side porch were made of the same canes. One big table was devoted to side dishes—Mexican peppers, salads, many dishes I couldn't identify, and a dishpan filled with cornmeal chips. The decoration for this table was a clear glass jug, about a ten-gallon one, that Mrs. Smith said she had bought sotol in (a Mexican intoxicating drink made from some weed that grows here). She had filled the jug with cane tops and painted a welcome sign on the side in English and Spanish. The other table was all barbecue and sauces and a couple of main dishes that were strange to me.

A Mexican band, with its git'tars and whatever else they use, came while we were helping ourselves to food. They played and sang in Spanish for the rest of the evening. People sat in small groups between the house and the river— some on the porch, sitting on the floor with a lantern in the middle of their circle, some on boulders, and some in chairs scattered about. Those of us away from the porch had no light except the soft twilight and the starshine. The river murmuring over the rapids and the sad Spanish music made the whole scene very western—sound and smell and taste very western. The men really do wear cowboy hats and look like movie cowboys. (I am so tickled on the playground watching the children playing kick ball with their western hats on. It's a matter of business with them—little and big wear those roll-brim hats.)

About three hours were devoted to eating, then the porch was cleared for dancing. People really got wound up then. One ardent cowboy, in boots and all accessories (no, not a gun), pressed me to come outside with him to cool off in the moonlight by the river. I kept politely refusing. Finally, he pulled me by the arm and insisted, "Come on. Let's go count the moon."

The Gibbs and I left soon afterward because they planned to get up early this morning to go to Alpine for the circus. Some of my children and their families were spending the night down there, camping on the river.

I was back home before ten o'clock. The grocery man from Marathon and his teen-age son (close friends of the Shollys who often spend the weekend here with them) came to deliver my week's groceries as they are going to the circus too and wanted to get an early start tomorrow with the Shollys.

The people up in the Basin are giving a barbecue next week, and they tell me that Mrs. Smith's barbecue is nothing compared to the Basin barbecue. I can't imagine that!

Take care and write. AK

SEPTEMBER 27, 1952

Dear Francys,

I've been in my apartment a week yesterday, enjoying myself immensely. Every night I put bread on my patio and wait for the skunks. The first night that I knew they were here I was studying at my table with my shoes off. I heard a scuffling, growling noise. I leaped up to see a small skunk fling itself out of the garbage box onto the floor of the patio, scratching and rolling. Ants in the garbage! Soon it disappeared around the corner and I rushed outside with a piece of bread. I sat on the edge of the patio, my bare feet on the one step, and broke up the bread all around me, so in order to eat it they would have to come close to me. Sure enough, here came the little one again hurrying around the corner, sniffing and sneezing like a cat. But instead of coming to the pieces of bread it came right to my bare feet. Nearer and nearer. I scrunched my toes tighter and tighter against the cement wishing I could scrunch them out of sight. When the skunk touched its long cool nose to my toes I visualized the sharp white teeth of the skunks in the Shollys' yard crunching dove bones, and I panicked. My toes flew up and hit the skunk in the face. Away it went with its tail straight up. I sat there waiting to be hit. (Some people become unconscious from the spray.) It didn't spray, but I was in almost as bad shape as if it had. Trembling, I collected the garbage it had pulled out and I stacked the two boxes, with the tops closed, tightly against the wall in the corner of the patio. They were heavy—my book boxes. Then I went inside.

In a few minutes I heard struggling, and angry meowing similar to a frustrated cat's noises. I looked out to see two enormous skunks strolling on my patio, and a large skunk tugging on one corner of the top box while the little one tugged on the opposite corner. They didn't succeed in dragging it down so the big ones went away. The little one stayed, and I watched him wrestle mightily with the box which I was afraid would fall on the creature and make him squirt my house. Finally he pulled the box down and dived into it, flinging garbage right and left. All that was sticking out of the box was the skunk's hind end and his long plumey tail. He was about a foot and a half from the door so I got the flashlight, eased the door open and examined his musk bags unbeknownst to him. There were two, one on each side under his tail.

Sunday Night—I've just come back from supper with the Gibbs family. I've put out my bread scraps for the skunks. One has now eaten his fill and left. They feel so relaxed while they eat that they lie on their stomachs with their tails stretched behind them and munch away.

Last night we went to another barbecue, in the Basin this time. Maggie Smith was there too. She told me about an orphan baby panther a Mexican brought her before its eyes were open. There had been two babies, a brother and a sister, but the brother died, and the sister was sick. The Mexican was afraid it would die too, so he walked a long way to bring it to Mrs. Smith because he thought she could make it well. She raised it on a bottle, named it Geneva, and had it so tame that every time she got out of Geneva's sight, the lion would whistle like a man until Mrs. Smith answered. But as it grew older, Geneva took a great dislike to children, and when the park asked Mrs. Smith to turn the lion loose, rather than risk Geneva killing or hurting a child, she gave it to the San Antonio zoo where it is now. AK

SEPTEMBER 30, 1952 - TUESDAY

Dear Jane,

I'm still not used to teaching in this school—it's wonderful. This morning I had only four children present. Two were absent due to illness. The other one, as it turned out, along with three children from Gertrude's room had a breakdown with their pickup which they drive forty miles every morning to school. About nine o'clock I looked out the window and saw them coming up the dusty, rocky road in their western hats and blue jeans and toting their lunch boxes and books. A kind man, they thought a "river rider" (a government employee who patrols the border), picked them up and brought them to Panther Junction. Two of the boys are fourteen (Jess) and sixteen (Bill) and have never been to school more than a few days in their lives. Gertrude and I feared they would disrupt our school, but I've never seen better-behaved, more cooperative boys. They work hard, and even in this short time they are doing second-grade work.

Teaching here is a lark compared with Alabama. Every day I marvel at the difference. I remember how strict my Alabama school was on the teachers— my principal was horrified to catch me drinking a cup of coffee another teacher gave me. Well, in the middle of a recent Big Bend morning, Mary Gibbs, mother of one of my sixth graders, strolled into the school in front of all the children with a steaming pot of coffee. The students continued with their studies while Mary, Gertrude, and I went to my apartment, joined shortly by the president of the school board who had come to fix a pipe. We took an enjoyable coffee break.

Mary came again at the close of school bringing a small chocolate pie for my supper. Sunday night she sent for me to come eat supper with her family. She washes my clothes and starches them; I iron at her house; she sends me quarts of buttermilk which she makes from Starlac powdered milk; she has given me rugs for my floors, a lamp to read by, and has done so much for me since I've been here I can't remember all of it. Things would have been a lot harder if I hadn't had her to look out for me. She has invited me to go to Alpine with her family Saturday, or a week from Saturday, whichever day they can go.

The scenery here is so beautiful it's a pity to stay indoors. I'm still in awe of it all. An Alpine woman who came by school the other morning told me about a friend of hers from Arkansas whom she brought to Big Bend for the first time. When the friend got out of the car and looked around, she exclaimed, "It's a lie! I don't believe it!" Those are my feelings exactly. Tonight I sat out watching the clouds and the mountains change after sunset until it was almost too late to prepare supper. The most beautiful mountain range of all is some distance away in Mexico and at every sunset it is rose-striped lengthwise—Sierra del Carmens it is called.

The skunks have already come and eaten their supper. Their bread bill is running up high. I thought they must be tired of brown bread—that's all I've fed them—so I ordered white bread for this week to provide some variety.

About sundown yesterday I was sitting at my desk working when a gray fox trimmed in red trotted past the window. Ten miles over the mountains in the Basin just the other night a large mountain lion strolled past the Chuck Wagon door paralyzing everybody who saw him. The deer over there appear in daytime, but over here they come out early morning, at twilight, and at night.

Bruce, a boy who lives in Panther Junction, has shown me an amazing bird nest in a cactus bush. It is made of straw, shaped like a bag lying on its side, and is eleven-and-one-half inches long. It's built about three feet above the ground and attached securely to the plant, almost as if it grew there. Sunday morning I went out before breakfast and made a sketch of it.

A monstrous spider lives in a corner of my bathroom. I don't have the courage to kill it so we just look at each other every time I go in there.

No, I'm not in a flood region here. It's so dry the whirlwinds blow everything away except the boulders. People tell me that sometimes there are short powerful rainstorms that flood these dry creeks and make driving dangerous, but since I've been here only about ten drops of rain have fallen.

I forgot to say how my ranch children got home. Their folks had no way to hear about their breakdown so didn't know they had no way home. Gertrude and I wrote a note to park headquarters asking if anyone were going toward the ranch at about three o'clock. Word came back that they would see that the children got home. At three a ranger came to school planning to take them to Persimmon Gap, which is about twenty miles from here. When he found out they had no way home from the Gap he was taken aback. He finally assured us he would take them on to the ranch even though it was far out of his way. AK

OCTOBER 1, 1952 - WEDNESDAY NIGHT

Dear Everybody,

Thanks but I have no use for the boots. It has barely sprinkled since I've been here and the rainy season ended September 30th. The park is full of what we call gullies in Alabama but which are dry creeks here. People say they become raging torrents when rain falls up in the mountains. On the dry, dusty, rocky seventy-mile stretch between here and Marathon you see things like giant yardsticks that measure higher than an automobile. They are flood gauges and made no sense to me until the people explained that they had to be there so that when one of these torrential rains has fallen the driver can estimate whether the water in the creek is too deep to drive his car through safely. Also if I wore boots here they would soon be shredded by this growth— various forms of cactus and a frilly-leaved shrub with very effective thorns— it's called cat claw.

I've been out on the patio with the skunks. Tonight they took bread from my hand. They are curious and walked all over my feet and sashayed up to the screen door and gazed inside. When I opened the door to come in for more bread one impudent little fellow came right after me as if he'd come inside. I shudder to think what I would do if he did get in.

I've spent a fortune on groceries setting myself up in the housekeeping business. We mail our grocery orders into Marathon on Wednesdays and Willie, the grocery man, delivers them to us on Sunday morning. Prices don't seem to be much higher than they are at home. AK

OCTOBER 7, 1952

Dear Everybody,

The Gibbs family went to El Paso yesterday and brought me back a Sunday newspaper, the first newspaper I've seen since I've been here. I was glad to check on the presidential campaign. I see it has gotten much more bitter since I last knew about it.

I have two more students now—the Mexicans whose father was stabbed. They are nicely spoken and well behaved. Since coming here I've met the first Mexicans I've ever known, and I'm well impressed. The janitor for the school is named Simon (See moan´). He is a good worker. He's employed by the park but cleans the school each afternoon after work.

My address is Big Bend National Park, so named because of the big bend the Rio Grande makes down into Mexico. I've found out there is no other county school in this, the largest county in Texas. The school board is giving me from December 19 to January 5 for Christmas, the longest holiday vacation I've ever had.

Every afternoon a fox comes to my skunk pan to drink. I'm patiently waiting for a lion to show up. AK

OCTOBER 13, 1952

Dear Francys,

I'll write you a note while I'm waiting for the men to unstop the school bathrooms. This is the second time they've stopped up this year—first time because a bulldozer ran over the pipe and broke it off so that dirt and gravel filled the pipe. This time I do not know. My bathroom is all right, probably because it isn't used much, but the boys' and girls' bathrooms have been a mess.

Now I have nine students—two in fourth grade, two in fifth, four in sixth, and one in seventh—but I've heard that we may have fifteen to twenty additions because a man just outside the park is building a tourist court and is importing the building crew.

A farewell party was held last Thursday night in the Basin for the superintendent and some others who are leaving the park. As I didn't know those who were leaving I partied with the children—twenty-one of them. The concessions manager donated enough prizes for every child to have one whether he won it or not. We had a fine time. A newspaper writer from Alpine, Glenn Burgess, attended the adult dinner. He came to our party too and made pictures of us in action. He also came to school next day and made pictures of students, teachers, and the school.

One night I was sitting against the patio wall when a little skunk walked over my feet smelling all around me. Four big skunks in the center of the patio pushed, shoved, and growled over the food. I don't know if the little one had eaten his fill or if he thought he'd play safe and wait till the others left. Anyway, after lingering around me he went to the other side of the porch and lay down against the wall, with his tail stretched out behind and his head on his paw like a cat. The big ones got ferocious, and some of them expelled

Miss Kilgore partying with the children of Big Bend National Park while the adults attended a farewell dinner party for the superintendent and several other departing residents.

warning scents. The little skunk jumped up and ran. Thinking he knew best, I got up and left too.

Tonight I am going with Mae, a clerk at headquarters, to Santa Elena Canyon. Ray, her friend who is visiting here, and Steve, her teenage son, are going too. We plan to cook supper down there. AK

OCTOBER 19, 1952

Dear Mary Alice,

I don't trust this mail system here. I sent my grocery order to the Basin post office last Wednesday, the day we are to mail our orders. Next morning, Thursday, it should have gone straight to Marathon where the grocer is. But Saturday (yesterday) when I went by the grocery store with the Gibbs family, my order hadn't arrived. When we came back by the store last night my order had come in the afternoon mail. So I'm wondering what happened to it during those lost days.

I bought myself a supply of magazines in Alpine. Today I've been catching up on the political news. It looks as if the presidential race is going to be close. I see that *Newsweek* says Sparkman is using his southern charm on the Ohioans.

Yesterday's trip to Alpine, 120 miles from the park, was my first. Mary Gibbs took me to many places and introduced me to many people. When someone from the park goes to town they carry lists, pick up packages, and run errands for other park inhabitants. Mary even made two long-distance calls for others, one to Chicago. We weren't home until nine o'clock and in the headlights of the car I saw one of my skunks running away from my apartment. They had no food and no water because I had been gone.

My water pan has attracted more and more customers. I've mentioned the fox that came every afternoon, a pretty, adult fox. It liked to lie on its stomach at the edge of the patio and take its time drinking. But one day the wind shook the schoolhouse doors so hard the fox jumped up and ran away. I haven't seen it since. Now I'm supporting gray quail that look like the ones at home except they aren't colored so richly, and black birds, along with the skunks.

Last weekend my students and I hiked to the top of a waterfall called the Window, a famous scenic spot. We had a lovely day and a fine walk down there. We could see between the two sheer mountains for a long way into Mexico. We ate our lunches there and hiked back a different way. We met part of a movie company that is filming a western named *Grubstake* in the park— the hero, the villain, and a father of one of my fourth-graders, Peter Koch, who is acting as guide, and several others. They were visiting various spots and taking trial shots with a new kind of camera that develops the film in a jiffy. They made our picture, developed it in fifty seconds, and the leading man, Larry, put a wax substance on it to make it permanent. It's posted in our schoolroom now. They invited us to come watch them work one day when they are shooting scenes for the movie.

The boys in our group insisted on leading us a terrible way back to the Basin. Straight up mountains: I could hardly hang on and most of the time I was on all fours. We left at 10:00 A.M. and staggered back at 4:10 P.M. We stayed not more than an hour at the Window. I enjoyed the hike but was exhausted afterward.

A "before" picture as teacher and students got ready to hike to the window. They were too weary for an "after" picture.

Next day I went horseback riding on one of the park horses with three of my students. My horse was a big gray, blind in one eye. Bloody tears oozed out of his good eye. I was so worried about his physical condition that I could hardly enjoy myself. We rode quite a way up the mountains through Juniper Flat and Boulder Meadow, lovely places. I expected to be gone only a short time and took nothing, but the children had a canteen of water and a lunch each. Before the trip was over I was swigging impartially from the canteens and munching any food I was offered—you know I was in poor shape to do that. I've learned now to take a hat, a canteen, and a lunch wherever I go even though I'm not supposed to be gone more than half an hour. That was an enjoyable expedition but I'm still sore from it.

The horsemanship I learned at Judson College is obsolete out here. On one expedition we were coming straight down a mountain; my horse was flinging his feet right and left and knocking down rocks—I could hear them hitting way below in the canyon. One of the girls was seated behind my saddle because the mule she had been riding bucked her off higher on the trail. She was clinging to me, and I was trying to dodge the tree branches. All of a sudden my horse went down in a hole, and I stayed up in a pine tree. When the tree let go of me I landed in the saddle again but my spectacles stayed in the tree. My horse would not whoa until all the horses halted. Then I dismounted and went back for my specs, which by this time had dropped out of the tree. They weren't broken but now they fit me crooked.

Everybody in Alpine was furious about the speech Stevenson made in Dallas Friday night. Texas tempers were flaring everywhere. I carefully kept my mouth almost shut. Write me. AK

OCTOBER 27, 1952

Dear Mama and Daddy, et al,

Your package came today. I was surprised at such a large one, and at so many nice things. The yellow tablecloth will be fine. I'm already using the notepad that was enclosed to make my next grocery list, and the cookie tin is dandy. The almanac I will probably keep for myself. It is certainly a deluxe edition, and a 1953 one this early! Bob Gibbs got some Spanish and English patent-medicine almanacs for the school, and we found out what we wanted to know about the morning and evening stars from them. I can hardly wait to read the *Newsweeks* and Pogo. I've missed Pogo almost—not quite—as much as I have you all. I've read both sides of the newspaper you enclosed.

At a park party Saturday night a visiting geologist, Ira Terry, turned out to be from Mississippi. He was familiar with Tuscaloosa and used to date a girl from Brookwood, he said. He couldn't remember her name though. He knew Weideman's Restaurant in Meridian and their black bottom pie. Last night Mary Gibbs had me over for supper. She said they had decided I got a course in geology the night before because Ira and I talked so long. I explained to her about where the man was from and how he was for Ike and was convinced Miss. was going Republican this year, and I said we both liked the same restaurant in Meridian that served such famous black bottom pies. She gasped, "Weideman's? (She pronounced it Weed-uh-man's). Every time we go cross country we route ourselves by Meridian so we can eat their black bottom pie." Mary has the restaurant's recipe given to her by the granddaughter of the man who first made the pie at Weideman's.

The Gibbses are being transferred to Isle Royale in Lake Superior. I don't know how I will get along without them. Just this weekend Mary brought me an ironing board she found at the Persimmon Gap ranger station and Bob brought me a porch chair so now I can associate with my skunks in comfort. Last night I had a delicious chop suey supper with them. At Isle Royale Bob will be superintendent. They do not know yet when they will leave but it won't be long.

Twice recently I've been down to Santa Elena Canyon, one of the show places of the park. One night we cooked supper there, and Saturday afternoon we fished and then cooked supper. We caught no fish. Both times I went with Mae who is a clerk in headquarters office, her son Steve, and her friend Ray from Odessa. Mae moved to Big Bend because of Steve's asthma. Steve is too old to attend our school. He takes a correspondence course. Last Thursday Mae went to the Boquillas ranger station on the river to give the ranger's wife a permanent. The ranger's wife, Mildred, invited me to come to supper too, and we surely enjoyed ourselves. The house is unusual and attractive, and across the river is the Mexican village Boquillas.

That was the night my small skunk had a tragic accident. We returned to my apartment about 11:30 P.M. Steve wanted to see my skunks, so we looked along the road to the school as we drove in. Always before I've seen a skunk somewhere along there at night but this night not a one was in sight. At my apartment we dumped a bag of scraps Mae had brought on the patio and then waited and waited for a skunk to come. Nothing moved anywhere. I told Steve I couldn't understand why not even one skunk was stirring. We finally gave up and they left.

I had just settled into bed about midnight when I heard a pitiful cry for help on the patio. I dashed out barefoot in my pink lace gown minus anything else except the flashlight. There by my door sat a monstrous owl taller than my knees clutching my small skunk that had squirted all over the porch. I hollered in a rage and beat the owl with whatever I could lay my hands on. How dare he! Each time I struck the monster he tried to fly away but couldn't lift off with the skunk. And no matter how I beat, he would not turn it loose. The owl managed to fly in spurts down the lecheguilla and cactus-infested hillside with me tearing out after him. (I took time to put on shoes). In the arroyo I found the owl had gone leaving behind my little skunk, limp but still breathing, its proud tail stretched out behind. I was scared witless that some varmint would drop out of the sky or leap from behind a creosote bush and nab me, so I grabbed my pet and ran back to the house as hard as I could. I laid it on the patio under a box fixed so that if it came to it could get out but the owl couldn't find it. I crawled back in bed but my house was so odorized I couldn't sleep. It got worse and worse. I couldn't breathe. I shut the windows, opened the air wick and set it on the floor right under my nose but it did no good.

Next morning, the skunk was gone. So was a large chunk of meat loaf I had laid at its nose hoping to revive it. Later one of the boys found my little skunk down the hill dead. My house was still unbearable. I scrubbed the porch several times with detergent but the odor lingered. Being desperate I poured undiluted Chlorox on it and that did the trick.

But the odor stayed with me personally. Every time I got low in the floor I smelled powerful skunk, not just in my house but wherever I was. Patty Gibbs suggested the scent might be on my shoes. I smelled of them. Yes! They were saturated where I had walked in the spray that night. Everyone says only time will remedy the situation. Tonight is the first night since then that I have had a skunk on my patio. The older, wiser ones must have sensed the owl was near that night. I am now supporting several foxes that seem to have dens behind headquarters in Horse Head Mountain.

In Alpine last Saturday Mary G. and I were talking to the Girl Scout secretary. She said that many of the ranchers expect to go broke this fall because of the low price of calves.

I'm getting along very well with my grocery orders. Forgot only once to mail my list on a Wednesday. Rather than let me go hungry, Willie looked at my past orders and made up a box of enough food to last till the next delivery. If I'm away when he delivers he puts my perishables in the refrigerator, a service I appreciate.

We're having a Halloween party next Friday for the park children—I'm on the committee. AK

NOVEMBER 9, 1952 - SUNDAY

Dear Daddy,

I enjoyed the clippings and also the newspapers. How was election night covered on TV? How late did you all sit up? Mary Gibbs' little boy Johnny and

Harold, a longtime ranger here, both had birthdays on election day. Mary invited Harold and me to supper that night. The Gibbs have a radio; otherwise I wouldn't have heard the returns. We had a wonderful supper—whole doves, biscuits, and other tasty things I can't remember at the moment. I was in dreadful suspense that Alabama would go Republican. I was the only one at the dinner party in favor of Stevenson. I thought well of his speech conceding the election but I didn't hear Eisenhower's reply.

Our Halloween party for the children was a great success. The Casa Grande Recreation Club (a park organization) gave Mary Gibbs and me $15 to buy gifts. The man in charge of concessions had already given us many little things that were suitable, and Harold brought us bags and bags of nice prizes he collected while on park business at the Texas State Fair. Every child ended up with too much to carry. We played games and enjoyed refreshments—cookies, Kool Aid, and candy. To top off the party the children went through the Basin (where the party was held) trick-or-treating and collected more treats at every house.

Tuesday, Nov. 11, we won't have school. I'll look forward to a holiday as I've spent most of this weekend washing and cleaning my house. The altitude does make a difference in the cooking here—at least, I hope that's what it is. I decided to bake beans. The longer I baked them the harder they became till after six hours I had a pot full of little rocks. Totally inedible.

Today I ate lunch at the Shollys' house—an all-Mexican meal and delicious. They also had the grocery man, Willie, from Marathon, and Rene, his wife, and Pat, the ranger from Boquillas (Boe-kee´us).

There is a great deal of social life here for such an isolated place. Or maybe it is more than usual because it is so isolated. I've two dinner invitations for next week plus farewell dinners for the Gibbs who are leaving the 24th.

Thursday was "Show Me" day in the park. People from Alpine and surrounding areas came down to visit and see what's here. All of them visited the school and oh-d and ah-d over it.

You should see my rock collection now. Harold, the-ranger-with-the-birthday, invited me to his house to see his collection, which is like something in a museum. Then he gave me a bushel basket full of all sorts of rocks that I've washed and put on a ledge around my room. For a long time the school has had a collection from the Smithsonian Institute which nobody ever bothered to unwrap. I hope to do a rock unit sometime this year but not soon, I think.

"Show Me" day, November 1952. Miss Kilgore stands in front of the window that overlooked an arroyo, park headquarters, the Dead Horse Mountains, and Sierra del Carmens. Photo by Glenn Burgess. Mrs. Gertrude is in the back by the blackboard.

You asked about the peccaries. Here the wild pig is the javelina which is pronounced have´a lee´ na. In pictures the two look alike, but I don't know if they are different. Everybody fears the javelina more than rattlesnakes. Maybe one reason is we have few trees anywhere to climb for an escape. Not even the one big skunk is left now. I guess the owl has caught them all.

I'll be glad to come home Christmas. Sigh. This place is most beautiful but not in the gentle way Alabama is beautiful. Everything is so unbelievably different out here. AK

NOVEMBER 11, 1952

Dear Mama,

I have been cleaning my house on this school holiday. I was just ready to wash when one of the rangers brought my mail and in it was the letter with the pictures from home. I was so glad to see them! I'll be there in just about a month now to see it all for myself. I know the fall colors must be beautiful there now. We have few trees here, but I've noticed some of the bushes up on Casa Grande are turning red. The weather is perfect however.

I went with Reece Sholly last night to K Bar Ranch where the Lundbergs live to the canasta party for this month. Most enjoyable though cards bore me to death. I spectated. The refreshments were most refreshing. I liked their fire too—a big fireplace with a fragrant cedar log on it. The house is adobe covered with a cement mixture. Towering all around it are piles of boulders (and rattlesnakes). The K Bar has its own windmill, hot and cold water, and a modern kitchen. Tonya and Carolyn, their older set of twins, are in my room.

Many farewell social affairs are scheduled in honor of the Gibbs family. The Shollys are having a dinner this coming Friday night for them, and Helen Minish is having a dinner on Saturday night, and there is a tea for them on Saturday afternoon. I will surely regret to see them leave.

Everybody in the park is involved in whatever goes on, it seems. A wedding is set for the last of this month in the community house (the old schoolhouse in the Basin) and I'm to take Mary Gibbs' place on the decorating committee as she will be gone by then. I've met the bride when I first came but haven't seen her since, and the groom helped Mary and me decorate for the Halloween party. I received an invitation to the wedding and have been asked to help serve refreshments.

I feel rich with all these towels and washcloths and aprons, etc., that you all sent. Everybody in the park knew what I got before I did because one end of the package was torn off. The president of the board, who picked up the mail that day, wouldn't accept the package until he inspected it and saw that it was all right. The package was well and strongly wrapped and nothing was damaged inside, just the paper torn off the end. Maybe somebody thought they might like to have what was in it until they saw it was household things. AK

NOVEMBER 30, 1952

Dear Francys,

I hope to leave for home December 20th at 8:20 P.M. from Alpine. It seems I've been away so long I can't remember what it's like there.

Friday I spent the night in the Basin. We decorated the old schoolhouse for a wedding and next day decorated the house for the reception. The cake was beautiful—one of the cooks at concessions made it. I helped mix the juices for the punch but one of the men did the spiking of it, using tequila. They say it is sickening mixed with fruit juices and sweet cake. Anyway, I heard no compliments on the punch, but there were plenty on everything else.

The drapes for my apartment finally came. Two of the boys helped me put them up after the wedding yesterday. The apartment looks more attractive, and I feel better not being exposed to the world, though I'm sure nobody would brave the cacti to spy through my window.

Thanksgiving Day I spent at Hot Springs and Boquillas Canyon with some people from the Basin. Then we came to my house to eat venison and hot biscuits for supper. I enjoyed the day, especially the company for supper. AK

DECEMBER 14, 1952 - SUNDAY

Dear Everybody,

The weather here continues beautiful. Dry, cool, sunshiny. Today was perfect and I had a most wonderful time. One of my student's family took me to a barbecue down at Lajitas, and we ate delicious food, listened to Mexican music played by a band, rode burros over into Mexico, explored adobe buildings in a deserted Mexican village, and collected some beautiful rocks.

I was sad the Gibbs were transferred, but I certainly garnered lots of invitations to dinners in their honor—one was a delicious Mexican dinner. All the women here are excellent cooks. It's hard for me to eat my own cooking after eating out so often lately. Before leaving, Mary gave a reception in honor of the new superintendent and his family, the Garrisons. It was a lovely affair. Everybody in the park came, and some people from ranches outside and even some from Alpine. I poured coffee, if you can imagine that—me sitting at a lace-covered table pouring coffee from a silver coffee pot.

Now is deer hunting season, and the rangers are on duty twenty-four hours a day at the two park entrances to see that no one shoots a park deer. When I went to Alpine with Mae and Steve we met many cars with the lovely creatures tied on top. One of my parents is sending me some venison tomorrow.

Gertrude Boulter, on the left, taught the lower grades. Miss Kilgore is in the center, and George Sholly, president of the school board, is on the right. Photo by Glenn Burgess.

Have I mentioned I am taking ballet lessons off and on? Etta Koch, one of my parents and wife of a photographer and lecturer who lives in the park, teaches a class for all ages every Friday night. Last Friday after ballet the Lundbergs, who live at K Bar Ranch about two miles from Panther Junction, invited me to go with them down to the Terlingua turn-off to visit with the ranger who was on deer patrol at that entrance. It was twenty or thirty miles down there, and what an isolated, pantherish-looking place it was. He was certainly glad to have company. He pumped up the little gas stove and made coffee, and we had cookies. His tent was lighted with an old-timey gas lamp, the kind that hisses while it burns. I kept looking in the shadows of the dirt floor for rattlesnakes. I didn't feel my house was so isolated after I saw his.

My children and I are planning a trip to McDonald Observatory, 135 miles from here, as a culmination of our Universe Unit. We are going in three cars. The observatory has the third largest reflecting telescope in the world, and it is in a beautiful mountainous area, they tell me.

Our new superintendent's wife, Inger, is a native of Alaska. She used to teach school near Juneau. They came here from Grand Canyon National Park. AK

JANUARY 19, 1953 - MONDAY NIGHT

Dear Mama,

I returned to the park January 2, and every day in Big Bend has been beautiful. On the following Sunday I went for a hike with Harold in the Grapevine Hills Canyon. I've never seen the like of it even in Big Bend—boulders, slabs of rocks, piles of stones everywhere you look. What barrenness, what grim beauty, what bizarre rock formations, and how huge they are! One called the Balanced Rock doesn't look balanced at all—a monstrous boulder way over my head barely caught between two weak-looking boulders. Just to stand near it for Harold to make my picture was scary. How he knew his directions or found his way back to the car after our hike is a mystery. I was glad to leave it behind. I can't recall seeing a live, growing thing in the entire canyon.

I just filled the water pan and put out food for my fox. The mountains were so beautiful in the sunset I had to linger a while to watch them, even though the air was a mite chilly. One fox comes to eat now, and quail and other birds, but no skunks anymore.

By the Wednesday after I returned to the park I had ground out seven of the twelve lessons on the Texas constitution and law that are required of me in order to teach here. Then came a letter from Sul Ross College begging my pardon but they had given me the wrong course. I was overcome. Thursday I took the day off and went in to Alpine with the president of the school board to see them. The man at the college gave me credit on the new course for the first four of the lessons I sent in, gave me the new book and the new questions, and I came back to begin over again. On Saturday I tossed off five lessons, went to see a slide show of the park that night that Harold showed the tourists, and spent the night with Mae in the Basin. Mae and Steve had breakfast with me next morning, but before they could leave and I could start work on my last lesson, Boots and Nealie Dott came and invited me to dinner and to visit a place on Tornillo Flat where a rhinoceros fossil was dug up and to drive on the old road alongside the Dead Horse Mountains to Boquillas and San Vicente on the river. I told the Dotts I could come if they'd let me bring my book and do the last lesson before we left for Tornillo Flat. I didn't see how I could miss a trip like that, job or no job, government or no government. While they fixed dinner I finished that last lesson. We had a delicious meal (Nealie makes a luscious chocolate cake using Irish potatoes) and a beautiful drive all afternoon. Returned to my apartment about eight o'clock loaded with rocks, deer horns, and odds and ends of treasures.

You can imagine how much I remembered about the government and the constitution by the time I took the exam Tuesday afternoon. I think I passed but haven't heard. But neither have I received my Texas teaching certificate. AK

FEBRUARY 9, 1953

Dear Everyone,

This day has been cloudy—that's unusual here—but we had one of the most beautiful sunrises and sunsets I ever saw. I walk late every afternoon in the foothills of the Chisos so I had an unlimited view and it was breathtaking. I don't believe there could be mountains anywhere as beautiful as the Sierra del Carmens in Mexico. They were memorable to see tonight. In front of them the Dead Horse Range and behind them the Fronterizas farther into Mexico. I can never get enough of looking at this country at any time of day.

Behind one of the hills where I walk I have been finding the most beautiful pieces of chipped stone unlike any I've seen anywhere else here. Harold, the ranger, says they are Indian chippings. The Apaches brought the stones from the flats and chipped them into weapons while they were camped in the Chisos. This afternoon I found a small, perfect arrowhead for shooting birds.

I see all kinds of birds over there and evidence of javelina rooting. I've found a whole deer skeleton where the lions had a feast (I keep hoping to see a lion), and I've seen many beautiful deer. No one else ever goes that way. How wonderful to walk alone and not be afraid some varmint (two-legged) might get me.

Yesterday was lovely but chilly. Harold and I took some sandwiches and went down to Dugout where the altitude is lower and the temperature much warmer. We built a fire and ate our supper. Dugout is one of the few places in the park where real trees grow—these are cottonwoods. In the soft spring-like wind their leaves twinkled beautifully, and the doves called mournfully. I was surprised to see how plants are budding down there—on January 22 when we went to Boquillas these trees were bare and silvery-white. Now they have bloomed and are making cotton bolls. Dugout is the old home place of Willie, our grocer. The park tore down the adobe house, made several fireplaces for tourists, and maintains a windmill there that pumps water into a square pond for animals and birds to drink. Willie tells exciting stories of when he was a boy there and Pancho Villa used to come over from Mexico on raids.

I love this country, and I'm enjoying being here immensely, but I'm thinking, come next summer, I'll move along. As yet I'm not legally teaching in Texas though. I gritted my teeth when another letter came from the state today. I'm to fill out the enclosed form and send them two more dollars (I've sent two already) and they promise to send my Texas certificate to me. Finally, last week I had word that I passed the Texas government course with a B. The president of the school board, who has sweated out the whole affair with me as he was one of the main ones responsible for hiring me, told me recently if I married I'd sure better marry a local fellow because he didn't intend to go through this with a new teacher next year. He said he expected me to be settled here for at least the next ten years. He grinned when he said it but there was some sincerity in it I know. Where will I get the courage to tell him if I decide not to come back next year? AK

FEBRUARY 9, 1953

Dear Jane,

How everybody loved those peanuts I brought from Alabama after the holidays! I gave one of the boys who comes to see me often a handful of them and he rushed away home. I was in the school working and Simon, the janitor, was cleaning when there came a loud, hurried knocking at the door. I looked at Simon, he looked at me. I wouldn't go to the door so he had to. In rushed a boy below school age, huffing and puffing. "Where's Miss Kilgore?" he demanded. "Jimmy said if I'd come up here she'd give me some peanuts." Simon pointed toward me at the other end of the room. The boy rushed over and hollered, "Will you give me some peanuts?" He was beside himself he had run so fast and was anticipating them so much. I gave him a handful, and he rushed away. He told me later that he roasted them.

What a blunder I made in school not long ago. I was walking past my two fifth-grade boys, and I smelled cookies. I thought they were sneaking a snack so I wrinkled my nose and said, "I smell vanilla flavoring." They both protested they were innocent, and they both added they were wearing the hairdressing I gave them for Christmas. I took a whiff of each head, and sure enough, that's what I smelled. AK

February 9, 1953 - Sunday Night

Dear Mama,

We have been having beautiful days here. Tonight is clear with a soft south wind blowing. I don't know what that may mean for tomorrow's weather. Many of the children have been out of school with measles.

Our trip to visit the Boquillas School made our students realize how fortunate they are. The teacher there, Señor Garcia (Gar-see´-ah), a Charles Boyer type, was very talkative and earnest in explaining things. Petra, in my sixth grade, and Bill, the sixteen-year-old first grader, were our interpreters. The school was in part of a chicken house—I peeked through a crack in the wall and saw chickens in the other half of the building. The students come from eight to ten miles away by foot, burro, truck, any way they can get there, he said. The school has no chalk and almost no material to work with. We have collected $2.50 that we are using to order white chalk, colored chalk, and an eraser for them.

Last weekend I went to Odessa with Mae. Odessa is a oil-boom town—very ugly, I thought, but we stayed with friends of Mae's who are Baptist. Next morning they not only got up and went to Sunday school and church but at each meal they asked the blessing and gave thanks, all of which is unusual out here at least among the people I know. AK

Dear Francys,

Happy day-after-Valentine. By this time I'm sure you've gotten my letter that was so long getting on its way because I mailed it without postage, unknowingly, and when it was sent back to me I had no cash to buy stamps. On my grocery list I ordered money to cash a check, it came, and I was able to buy stamps again.

Willie, the grocer, is wonderful. The school ordered a box to use for Valentines, and he brought us a nice one. Two weekends ago I went to Odessa with Mae. Willie put all the perishables in the refrigerator for me and stacked everything else neatly. If there's something on a grocery list he doesn't have, he goes shopping for it and usually finds it. A great convenience—the only thing is you must think a half a week ahead to get the list in to him.

Thanks for the information and addresses you sent. I'm going to write and apply to the schools this coming week. I've about made up my mind not to come back here next year, though they've been wonderful to me for the most part and I've loved being here.

I have not been sick at all, though many of the children have been out of school with the measles. We've had only two cases of flu.

I'm just back from a reception at the superintendent's home for our new assistant superintendent—an enjoyable affair. I went late and was invited to stay for a buffet supper. When I was home Christmas I bought a pretty gray-beige dress, pleated all over and with grosgrain ribbon at the waist. It is wool mixed with a new material that holds the pleats in, and it is washable. I wore it with some of Aunt Bessie's jewelry—I like it very much.

You remember that French novel Aunt Bessie bought for me? Ray, Mae's friend from Odessa, was shocked when he saw it on my bookshelf, and Harold, a ranger who comes to see me sometimes, raised his eyebrows sky high when he saw it. "Quite a girl," he said, meaning, I think, Madame Bovary, not me. I must get around to reading it.

One night recently Steve, Karen, and I had Harold to supper at my apartment. Steve is fourteen and was spending the day with me while Mae was in Alpine. Karen, twelve, is in my seventh grade. Mama always groans when I'm in the kitchen at home because I'm so slow. She would have given up if she had been around the three of us concocting the meal. Steve and Karen are worse than I am, and with the apartment so small, we had a confusing time. We began cooking at three, and we still weren't ready when Harold came at six. But everything was tasty. I fixed that chicketti recipe of Mary Gibbs'—it must be foolproof if I get delicious results with it. Steve made the biscuits while I was dressing in the bathroom. I heard Karen ask him if he wasn't supposed to put some milk in them. He had forgotten that and had put nearly a pound of shortening in the flour trying to make it stick together. After they were cooked, I accidentally dropped a biscuit on the floor and it shattered into crumbs it was so rich, but we ate them politely. AK

FEBRUARY 22, 1953 - SUNDAY NIGHT

Dear Everyone,

This has been a beautiful day, though cold in the wind, and a most exciting weekend altogether. Yesterday morning as I was hanging out my wash the Dotts (Boots, Nealie, and their three boys: Jack, Millard Ray, and Jimmy) came by on their way to San Vicente and Boquillas, the Mexican village where delicately colored florespar ore is brought over the border (and where the school is we visited). Without hesitation, I left my wash and had a most enjoyable time. Even though the dust in the air dimmed the mountains, they were still beautiful. The river was low—no rain in so long—and we drove through it with no trouble.

At the meat market in Boquillas the butchers were cutting up two white-faced calves, fat and clean looking, though the men were working on what looked like very polluted ground. Boots bought a hindquarter of beef at twenty cents a pound. At San Vicente we browsed through Maggie Smith's store. (She has moved from Hot Springs). She had many new things she had bought from a store in Marathon that went out of business—nothing outstanding for women, but beautiful 3X Stetson hats, which Boots says are the best, for $9, originally $25. They are the stockman's style, and Boots urged me to send one to you, Daddy. Are you interested? One was a pale green. They are quite the thing around here but I don't know about in Alabama. I almost bought one for myself they were so pretty.

We had a park party last night in honor of George Washington. I think I
have never enjoyed a grown-up party so much. I know I have not ever danced
so much in one evening. We were not back to Panther Junction until three-
thirty in the morning, and I was not in bed until four, but maybe a night like
that once a month is not damaging.

I am enclosing the article by Glenn Burgess that appeared in the *Fort
Worth Star-Telegram* recently about our school. I'm also sending a box of Indian
chippings, Comanche or Apache, that are beautiful. They came from the
Chisos Mountains (Chee´sos, meaning phantom or ghost) near the school. As
you all usually have bulbs of some kind I thought these would be pretty to put
in the bulb bowl, as well as interesting historically. Water makes the colors
even brighter. In his rock collection Harold has a jar of them that he keeps
filled with water. I keep mine in a metate, a bowl carved out of stone that the
Mexicans use for grinding peppers and garlic. It is three-legged, like an iron
pot, and has a grinding rock, a *manos*, to hold in your hand. I bought it in
Boquillas. The small rocks among the chippings that look like purple glass are
florespar as are the yellow glassy ones. Florespar comes from about seventy-five
miles down in Mexico and is used as a flux in making steel, they say.

A holiday for the school tomorrow—I hope to catch up on my schoolwork.

February 25—Our power plant here at Panther Junction failed sometime
last night. No lights when I got up this morning, and my refrigerator was
defrosted. We had the heaviest fog I have ever seen anywhere. Without the
power plant our school furnace didn't work, so the school was very cold.
George (president of the board) came up about 9:30 to inquire about us. Since
the children, especially the little ones, were cold, and it would be two or
three hours before the plant could be fixed, he told us to send them home. A
holiday! Tra la! As the Basin pupils commute with Gertrude, the other
teacher, and Bill, the first grader, drives the ranch pickup, we had no transportation problems.

Where are the months going? I can't believe that February is over and
done with already. A new school board will be elected in April. By then I must
decide if I want to return next year in case the new board offers me the job
again. One day I think I do; the next I know I cannot. If there were only a
church to go to, and I think of the ballet, and once in a while a movie and a

play, and museums, and concerts, etc. that I could go to if I were in a city. Sigh. We do have ballet lessons over in the Basin taught by Etta and attended by boys, girls, and me. And sometimes when an artist visits the park and stays for a prolonged period, he will organize classes, but I've not tried painting.

In school we are learning the cutest song now about a fellow who lived on the Tombigbee River and made himself a gumtree canoe. I love to sing it, and so do the children. I told them the Tombigbee is practically in my backyard in Alabama. The other teacher plays the piano, which adds so much to our enjoyment of school.

The Basin, a thousand feet higher than we are, had a sprinkle of snow last night. From the looks of the clouds I expected snow at Panther Junction, but already the sun is beaming down and the sky is clearing. AK

FEBRUARY 25, 1953

Dear Francys,

Enclosed is my application to the San Diego City Schools. Will you mail it for me? My mail goes in and out of the president of the board's office, and I'd rather he wouldn't know yet that I'm applying for another job.

We have had our first wintry weather this week. Yesterday the fog was so close and thick I couldn't see five feet away. Our furnace wasn't working. The children were so cold, at George's suggestion we sent them home. Mae and Etta came across the arroyo from headquarters for lunch with me. We had an enjoyable time. Sunday I had a most wonderful time with Etta, her family, and some others at Oak Creek, down toward Santa Elena Canyon. It is an old ranch place and very beautiful. (I think so now but wouldn't have last August.) We had thick steaks broiled over oak coals and coffee. It smelled as wonderful as it tasted. The sun was golden and warm. I can taste, feel, and smell it all now. We found a place full of beautifully colored Indian chippings, and I added to my collection. Today I mailed a box of chippings home, along with some purple and yellow florespar I picked up in Boquillas, across the border, last Saturday. I thought they would be pretty to grow bulbs in, and historical. They came from the Chisos Mountains just behind the school. Comanche Indians. AK

Dear Jane,

Sunday is the day I miss home the most and think of you all more, no matter what I do. Sunday is just a holiday from work here—no church, no Sunday school even for the children since the Gibbs left.

For today Etta and Pete Koch had invited me to go with them through Mariscal Canyon in rubber rafts. It was to be an all day affair with lunch. (In some places, the Rio Grande is so shallow and rocky you have to get out and carry the rafts while everybody wades.) Everything was ready. Willie, our grocer, and his wife Rene came down last night, and Willie's helper, Juan, was to bring the park's groceries and deliver them for Willie this morning, as we expected to be away to the canyon by 6:30. Well, it's the first time since I've been here that I've known the weather to interfere with plans. But in the last week we've had much dust in the air—blowing over from New Mexico, they say—visibility has been limited. Then the weather turned quite cold. I hung my washing out yesterday morning, and in a few minutes I looked out and saw icicles along the bottom of the bedspread like tassels. Word came to me in the afternoon that the men of our group had gotten together and decided the weather wasn't suitable—winds in the canyon would be high, and what with wading and the icy weather, the trip wouldn't be wise. We were very disappointed. Willie was the most crushed of all. He said he had worked since five o'clock yesterday morning getting his orders for the park filled and had gotten Juan to give up his day off for the trip. Then too we had all the food the Kochs had ordered.

So Etta decided we'd have a picnic today. At eleven o'clock, the Kochs radioed from the Basin to Panther Junction to meet them at Government Springs at one-thirty and we'd go to Oak Creek, far down toward Santa Elena Canyon. It is at the foot of a sheer two-hundred-foot drop called the Window because two mountains frame it. When the rains come a gorgeous waterfall pours down from above. Last fall my students and I hiked to the top of the Window, but I'd never been to the base before—it is wild and beautiful. The old two-story ranch house is still there, and a pond of water, and a hill full of Indian chippings. We drove through what they called a "trap," but what is really a cactus-filled pasture. Four cute burros stood in the cactus gazing at us. George, the chief ranger, and his son Danny got out of the car, and one burro let George walk up to him and mount. After George got the burro out of the cactus, he put Danny on him and down the road to our picnic place they went in front of the car—George walking behind with a stick and Danny riding bareback, guiding the burro by tapping his neck. They both had to beat him every once in a while to keep him moving, but he provided entertainment for the children the whole afternoon.

We built a fire and had it going by the time the other two cars arrived. Pete broiled the most luscious thick steaks over the coals and made a big pot of coffee. Everybody here takes their coffee black, and they've declared with certainty that I will too before I leave Big Bend. I don't think I ever can. Yet it is a mighty inconvenience to have sugar and cream brought along just for me. That second pot of coffee was so black and bitter I don't see how they downed it straight. But it was wonderful sitting around the fire, leaning against the rocks and logs, in the lovely sunshine where the wind couldn't reach us and the beautiful hazy blue mountains in the distance. We all agreed that it did make up completely for our lost canyon trip.

On the way back we saw a fox sitting in broad daylight near the road watching us, and a group of thirteen deer that looked at us curiously. Seven antelope, more beautiful than deer to me, ran along the road with us for quite a way. It was just past five o'clock, and the drive home was most beautiful. I know that I shall never be any place that I shall love more than this—it cannot be described with justice. It is hard for me to understand how I felt when I first saw it! AK

MARCH 10, 1953

Dear Mama,

Sunday night we had the only real rain since I've been here—a soaking one and lots of lightning and thunder. It caused some problems. Our mailman got stuck on the road at the west entrance to the park, near Terlingua. As a result yesterday's mail was delivered late. Our students from out on the ranch couldn't come to school because the creeks were up. We leave to Bill, the first grader who is their driver, the decision as to whether it's safe for them to come to school or not. Also, when a cloud comes up during school, if Bill says they need to go home, they go. These creeks are all dry until a rain, and then they are torrents feared by everyone except the drunks or the ignorant. I was in Alpine Sunday with Mae and Steve when the rain began. As we sped down the road that night toward the park we could see the dark clouds and lightning hanging over the mountains. We were sure Tornillo Creek would be up and we'd have to spend the night waiting for a chance to cross. But we beat the water to our crossing and got safely home.

We had an enjoyable day, but I was surely weary. We had gone in early and visited a friend of Mae's. Then we lunched at the Little Mexico Cafe where the Mexican food is excellent. In the afternoon Mae's church (Jehovah's Witness) had a meeting at her friend's house. All of their members I've met are hard working and sincere and many of them are young, but I cannot accept their beliefs at all. The young man who spoke Sunday gave an interpretation of the fall of Adam and Eve that I'd never heard before. He said the serpent appealed to the weaker of God's two created beings, Eve, and succeeded in leading her astray. Then when Eve asked Adam to eat of the fruit, Adam saw she had already disobeyed God and that she would be punished, so he, noble soul, ate of the fruit too so that he could be wherever she would be and suffer whatever consequences she suffered. The leader didn't explain why when God called Adam to account, he quickly blamed it all on Eve.

Friday night I went to the river with the Dotts to take food to Nealie's brother who was down there fishing. He was camped in a dobie house amongst the tarantulas and rattlesnakes. The night was balmy and beautiful with a soft breeze blowing. The fellows built a fire, made coffee, and we had cookies while we talked. Nealie's brother's name is Woody. He's the one I told you all about who grieves because he didn't live back in the days of the Old West. He is long and lean and wears tight, bowlegged jeans and a Texas hat. He loves fishing and hunting, but this weekend he didn't catch a thing.

On Saturday I spent the day with the Dotts and their guests from Iowa. We went to the Gulliher ranch (pronounced "Gullyhair"), away over in the Rosillos Mountains. The Gullihers were shearing sheep and mohair goats. For two weeks they had been rounding up the critters from the far corners of the ranch. The shearing crew had come just that morning. They used a noisy machine with six men working on each side of it using big clippers. The men worked rapidly, without pausing between animals. For every animal they shear, they get a metal chip as the wool grabber gathers up the wool. They are paid according to the number of chips they have on their string.

The poor animals, with the men's knees in their bellies and their necks bent backward, rolled their eyes up in their heads and cried most pitifully. Because of the men's haste, the sheep suffer many cuts and are bloody. Often after shearing, when the sheep are naked, a cold wave comes and how they suffer then.

Certain goats are trained to lead the sheep into the shearing pen. The sheep trust the goats and follow them in. Then the goats leap over the fence of the pen and frolic on the stuffed woolsacks until time to lead another batch of helpless victims into the pen. The poor sheep are subjected to the pain and indignity of the shearing. But I had to laugh at the goats—they so obviously realized their superior station in life and had such a good time between their assignments.

The head of the shearing crew was an older man called "el Capitan." I asked him to pose for me at the fire where the crew's supper beans were cooking in a big pot. To add interest to the picture I asked him to lean over and stir the beans, which was a social error. Stirring frijoles was beneath el Capitan's status, I realized later.

A grandson of Grandpa Gulliher, Rowdy, just home from Korea, was there. He had been stationed at Camp Rucker, Ala., for six months and disliked it so much he asked to be sent to Korea. He took the Iowa visitors and me on a tour of the ranch in a pickup. He didn't need a road—he'd take out across the lecheguilla and rocks to go wherever he wanted. Coyotes had been killing their sheep, he said, and he showed us a trap they had set at a dead sheep. We saw the coyote's tracks all around the carcass but it hadn't touched the sheep or the trap.

An odd custom at the ranch is the way they eat meals—the women serve the men from the kitchen, the men all sit together in the main room that is decorated with guns and antlers, the men in chairs, the younger males sitting on the floor against the wall. The women then eat together sitting around in the kitchen. They never mingle during mealtime, and the conversations they carry on are totally unalike.

Last weekend I had a wonderful time at my fifth grader's family ranch. The Carrolls are new here, came from Missouri, and plan to build a motel for tourists. We went to a burro basketball game in Marathon, toured Dog Canyon on foot and explored Indian caves, went to a quicksilver mine, collected rocks from the dry bed of Maravillas Creek (my apartment floor is still full of rocks—haven't had a chance to put them away), and one night made a 240-mile round trip just to see a movie. That was incredible to me but means nothing out here. Bill and his brother, Jess, and their family live on the ranch too.

I am sending a long story from the paper about a mountain lion chasing a little girl. I thought it uproariously funny, but when Boots, a Texan himself, read it he didn't crack a smile. I asked him why not because it had tickled me very much. He said he thought on the serious side of the story—a good Texan nearly losing her life.

Got to hop in bed. AK

MARCH 14, 1953

Dear Mary Alice,

Here we have had a real rain, and the desert and mountains are greening and blooming all over. On the 11th I went to Alpine with the Kochs through hail and rain to see a troupe of Spanish dancers, an energetic program with beautiful costumes. Driving back to the Park at 2 A.M. we mowed down the joyful jack rabbits that were dancing en masse in the moonlight—thump, thump, knock, every other second, with us laughing hysterically and crying at the same time. I wouldn't look back, but I know the road was littered with jackrabbit bodies. No way could we avoid them!

Our school is out June 5th. If I take this job next year, or if I'm offered it, I'm thinking I'll come home and start work on my master's degree. I long for the things of civilization sometimes, but once I leave here, I'll probably never come back, and there are so many experiences I've had here that I couldn't have anywhere else, sometimes I think I'd better stay another year while I'm about it. The only thing is—the longer you stay in the Big Bend, the tighter it binds you to itself.

I think I will never get used to the ways of the people here—casual—or something. No day is ever routine. I wrote you all about our power plant failing and George, the president of the board, sending the children home because the school was so cold. Then the other day the children and I were working away when the door opened, and George, without a word, beckoned me to come outside. I looked at the children, they looked at me. I went, and there on the porch floor stretched out on a paper was a nine-foot (from nose-tip to tail-tip) panther hide with blood still wet on it. His head was there and his paws. He was lovely, like a monstrous tomcat, with scarred ears, very long claws, and paws larger than my hands. A rancher in the Rosillos Mountains had been after him for a year and had just now killed him. After I recovered, we called the children to look him over. Many of them have seen the real thing often but always alive. Bill and Jess from the ranch have hunted them. The children were horrified when I said I would raise sheep just to feed panthers because they are so handsome. I have learned to say what I want in Border Spanish: *Un lion chichita viva*—a little lion alive. I knew to add the "alive" part because the ranchers are death to lions.

Which reminds me that on that very morning, when I had crawled out of the bed at 6:30, with my eyes still half-shut and my pink lace nightie dragging about my feet, there came a low growl from my dark patio. I nearly dropped the coffee pot. I couldn't move. In a few seconds came another growl, this time from inside the school, right at my door. Now I could recognize that it was a human voice growling so I said, hoping to get an answer in English, "Now who in the world is that at 6:30 in the morning?" The only answer was another growl. Sometimes one of the little Mexican girls has to come early but she has always been quiet like a mouse so I knew it was not Juanita. The tone of the growl sounded like Danny Sholly, but I looked across the arroyo at his house and saw no lights. I didn't think his family could even be up, and I knew they would never let him escape to school at that hour. I couldn't get any response but growls from "it," so I tried to eat my breakfast. "It" began throwing itself on the door and turning the doorknob. I was sure "it" was a child but couldn't imagine how or why at such an hour. I wouldn't have opened the door for anything in the world though to see what "it" was. Then I heard the outside door open, movement away from my door, and there were no more growls or noise of any kind. Later at school I asked Danny about it. He wouldn't say a word, just grinned. Later still I found out he had spent the night over in the Basin with the Kochs; they brought him home at 6:30. He crept in his house, got his books, and came to school while his family was still in bed. His mother, Reece, when she discovered he was gone, looked out the window and saw him moving about the school grounds and sent George for him. Law me! I grew a gray hair over that.

Then just recently we were working away, when the door opened and I turned around to see Harold. The children were delighted. They have really teased me about him. (There is no such thing as a private life here). He was just back from vacation and had some pictures he wanted to show me. He was very casual and the children were included in his conversation. (He has half-raised them all, he says). In front of the children, he invited me to go on a picnic with him. I was overcome. The children were tickled to death. I have been telling them, every time they mentioned Harold during school hours, that I don't mix business with pleasure and that school is business, and they were just about convinced I was right. But now I knew I had lost all I had gained in that way. I would work and talk my head off trying to get a point over in history—I'd think the children were completely absorbed in what I was saying and were with Magellan down at the tip of South America or I would be carried away by some other great moment in history, but when I'd pause for their reaction one of them would say, "Where did you and Harold go last night?" or one would glance out the window and say, "Yonder goes Harold." One afternoon I was working on a great stack of papers, checking as fast as I could on Eligio's spelling sentences. He had made nice, meaty fourth-grade sentences, and I was ready to give him an "E" when I read his seventeenth sentence using the word "wonderful": "The date was wonderful last night, Harold," he had written. I almost fell out of my chair. Our friendship is more world-shaking to them than it is to either Harold or me. It is not good that this should be so, but I do not know now how to change it.

When I went out to take my daily walk late one afternoon two of the small boys saw me and asked if they might go along. I told them no, please, I'd rather go alone. They said they'd come anyway, that I was going to meet Harold, and they wanted to see him too. I told them no, I had been with them in school all day and I needed to be by myself now and I didn't want them with me. But they followed me all the way, and I really went miles. Way over on the edge of an arroyo I finally sat down on a big rock. They sat down, puffing, on another rock on a hill above me. "Hello," they called. I ignored them. They tried to get a conversation started. I still ignored them. The sun set, dark began to come. I made no move to go, so they finally crept away. I was most annoyed.

When I went to the Gulliher ranch over toward Nine Point Mesa with the Dotts and their Iowa guests the other weekend we were standing together in a corral when Grandpa Gulliher and Fred with a group of men I didn't know showed up. I was admiring the horses and noticing the leather chaps and spurs, which I didn't believe cowboys really wore nowadays, and their boots, and I wasn't paying much attention to the others until suddenly Fred pounced on me, bellering, "What the devil's yore name now?" I stared at him speechless. He hadn't shaved or bathed or had a haircut since they started rounding up the sheep and goats two weeks before. His wild hair poked out every which-way from under his hat, his eyes were red and weary under his shaggy eyebrows, and his beard unkempt. I realized he probably wanted to introduce me to the other men, but I just stood there. Nealie answered for me. Can you picture that happening in Alabama? I had told Rowdy Gulliher that one reason he disliked Alabama so much was because the people are more reserved than Texans are, and there is an example. AK

MARCH 15, 1953

Dear Daddy:

Yesterday was beautiful here. The sun shone all day. Panther Junction was cool, but some of us went down to Lower Hot Springs, where it was very hot, to spend the day. We hiked over the trails to see the cactus plants that are blooming now. The ocotilla is beautiful and plentiful, long spines broken out in scarlet blossoms. The spring where people used to bathe (the park doesn't allow bathing now) has a stone bathtub and is very pretty. I discovered the water is warm, not hot as the name implies. A Mr. Langford, who homesteaded at Hot Springs, has written an interesting book called *Big Bend* about his life at Hot Springs. We climbed straight up a hill to the ruins of his house. What a view he had up and down the river. His outhouse hangs over the cliff and is built of flagstones.

We made a fire on the rock floor of a house at the lower spring and had tortillas for lunch—a flat cake of meal, thinner than a pancake, fried quickly in shortening, sprinkled with cheese, lettuce, and onions, with hot sauce poured over it. They were good but all that onion and heat made us too sleepy and energyless. Etta Koch and Reece Sholly, the two parents leading our expedition, had intended to draw pictures of river scenes but not a one did they do.

The river rider came along on his horse patrolling the border. He keeps Mexican cattle from crossing the river and bringing over diseases. He made a dashing figure wearing his uniform, big hat, and gun. His horse shone to perfection. It had a Mexican name I can't remember, but the river rider said it means "monkey." After talking with him, I believe he leads a lonely life, as do many people down here in the Big Bend.

Bill and Jess, the boys from the ranch, used to have an adult deer they had tamed when it was a fawn. They let it roam free, but it never went far from home and would always come when called. One day when the deer was out near the road, a car stopped and two men jumped out. They shoved the deer into the back seat of the car and sped away. Nobody was near enough to stop them or get a tag number, and the deer never came home again.

A beautiful tree we've come upon beside the dry creeks is called the "poor man's orchid." It is small with no noticeable leaves and festooned with lavender-purple blossoms like an orchid.

I think of the overflowing wells we have in Alabama, a never-ending gush of clear water. The springs out here are different—few and far between and very skimpy flowing. One on the way to the Gulliher ranch has a sign posted that warns the water is "poison." Another one is called "Dripping Springs," and the Dotts live at one named "Government Springs."

Boots Dott is an old cowboy, though he works for the park now. One time out on the range far from any doctor, he crawled into his sleeping bag after a hard day and was bitten by a black widow spider. The outfit's cook fixed him a poultice of kerosene to tie on the bite. Boots fell asleep and next morning had no ill effects other than a blistered leg where the kerosene poultice had been. AK

MARCH 17, 1953

Dear Francys,

Thanks for mailing my letter to the San Diego City School System. The reply was prompt. I returned the application to them yesterday. The procedure for getting California credentials is very complicated—health exam,

Miss Kilgore takes a drink at the Carroll Ranch before going down to the Maravias creek bed to hunt rocks.

Two thirsty hikers take a drink from a puddle in Dog Canyon. No telling how old the water was and how flavored with sheep droppings.

fingerprints, a course in U.S. Constitution (groan! another one of those) and much else, but the beginning salary is $3400 as I read the salary schedule. I make $2600 here this year. That would be quite a jump up.

The weekend I spent at the Carroll ranch on the Marathon road we went exploring in Dog Canyon. The children (the two big boys in our school, Bill and Jess, their sister, and Raymond, my fifth grader) enjoyed themselves immensely because I was so ignorant, I think. (At one meal we had a delicious meat dish that they claimed was "Gopher Stew.") I pulled a dreadful boner. We were rambling in Dog Canyon, hunting rocks, exploring the caves, and visiting an Indian camp. On our way home in the pick-up Bill said, "Here is the best place to find pretty agates." He stopped, and we hopped out. We were all intently searching, with me exclaiming and admiring and the children bringing choice specimens to me, when I sighted something at my feet partly hidden by dirt, like a half-submerged gold nugget. "Oh, my," I hollered. "What in the world is this marvelous thing?"and I bent over it in awe. Everybody came running to gather 'round me and stare. Silence. Then Raymond, in an uncertain voice, said, "That's something that came from the inside of a sheep." A sheep dropping! How quietly we scattered and began looking for agates again. And I kept my mouth shut until I was sure what I was hollering about too. I'm not over it yet.

Something else I can't get over is how casually the children drink water from any source—the Rio Grande, a stagnant pool in a creek, or a puddle in a canyon. In Dog Canyon, Bill took off his sombrero, knelt, and drank a cupful of water that had collected in the rocks not far from where I later discovered my gold nugget.

Last week we went in to Alpine to a wonderful program by Rey and Gomez, Spanish dancers on tour. How I did enjoy the dances, costumes, and the pianist and his solos. We weren't back to the park until 2:00 A.M. which made it difficult to get up to another day of teaching, but so worth it! AK

MARCH 24, 1953

Dear Francys,

Sunday afternoon with Mae and Steve I hiked up Wright Peak, the middle one behind the school. Away up on the side we made a fire and cooked our supper. How beautiful it was. We walked down the mountain in the moonlight hoping we might meet a panther—no luck.

Last week a woman tourist with her child was strolling up a mountain from the Basin and met a lion. She and her little girl ran back down the mountain to her husband, screaming all the way. Concessions people said you could hear her in the Basin. The little girl left her sweater behind; the husband didn't believe they saw a lion. He went for the sweater and met the critter coming down the trail after the woman and child. He vamoosed too. I may have a chance yet. AK

MARCH 29, 1953

Dear Everybody,

Juanita, Petra, and Raymond had to stay inside during play period because they had fooled around and not done their work. When the rest of us came back inside, they had vanished, but written on the board in large letters was this message:

Notice!!

Dear Miss Kilgore,

We have gone to Marathon. We are going to catch a ride with the ore trucks.

Goodbye,

Juanita, Petra, and Raymond

I didn't go looking for them. I didn't have time. But I was well aware of the huge trucks passing on the road to Marathon, loaded down with the ore they haul from the mines farther down in Mexico. I just trusted that the students were pranking and would eventually return. Sure enough the three of them soon came shuffling in from wherever they had been hiding (down in the arroyo I expect).

Etta says you aren't a real Big Bender until you've stayed all night on the wrong side of a creek bank waiting for the water to go down low enough to cross over. She sat one night until 2 A.M. beside Maravillas Creek, reading the newspaper by flashlight. Boots says to keep safe you must watch for the cloud of dust that precedes the wall of water as it moves down the dry creek bed.

Last night as I sat on my porch I noticed a Spanish dagger in beautiful bloom at the fox water pan. Later while I was ironing I heard hoofbeats—deer. This morning no trace of my dagger blossom was left.

One afternoon Mae and Steve came over from the Basin to take me to see a white pitaya they had heard was in bloom out toward Persimmon Gap. None of us had ever seen a white one. Most commonly pitayas are a deep rosy red and are sometimes called "claret cup" because of the color. We had exact directions, though there are few landmarks in the area where the plant was supposed to be, and we wandered about quite a bit. By the time we found it, sure enough it was white, but there wasn't enough light left for us to make pictures.

Many people from the park regional office and from the national office in Washington come and go here. Those I've met are quite interesting (paleontologists and historians, for instance). One time I rode into Alpine with such a visitor. We had an enjoyable time chatting about all sorts of things, mostly the park and the way we live. Toward the end of the trip I remembered something I had wanted to ask him. "Do you know anybody who drinks Jack Daniels whiskey?" Silence. He turned to look at me, disregarding the perils of a Big Bend road, as shocked as if the schoolteacher had made improper advances. I hurried to explain why I wanted to know—Jack Daniels whiskey comes in beautiful bottles like cut glass and I wanted somebody's empty bottle for my own. He didn't know a Jack Daniels drinker. AK

Dear Jane,

Today we had a few drops of rain out of two different clouds—some thunder but no lightning that I noticed. The wind is blowing hard and gusty now. I hope things calm down before morning as tomorrow is the park's big picnic down at Santa Elena Canyon. I am going with the Dotts and Gullihers (from the ranch). It will be an adventurous day with all of them.

The Shollys are having everyone from Panther Junction to their house for Easter breakfast at nine o'clock. If the wind isn't blowing too hard Reece wants to have it in her yard, which is very pretty with flowers and greenery—it is securely fenced in from the deer.

Today was election day for the new board of trustees. I spent the night in the Basin with Mae and meant to have a look at the polling place as we came out this morning but forgot. It would be interesting to know who our new bosses are—probably I could judge if I will be offered the job again next year if I knew. The newspapers say that Texas teachers are practically assured of a $600 raise next year. I've caught the knack of teaching four grades—it would be much easier for me next year. I'm very fond of all ten of the children, and it would be nice to come back to a place where I know people rather than plunging into another new place. But I've applied to San Diego schools— salary $3400 a year to begin with (I get $2600 now).

At last I have help with the Girl Scouts here. The new ass't superintendent's wife, Irene, has taken over leadership, and I'm her assistant as I was with Mary Gibbs. That takes a load off me.

I was discussing the price of a burro with one of the park men the other day. He nearly fell off the mountain when I told him that you all are trying to save $5 to buy a burro. He said, "Shhhh!" looking all around to make sure nobody heard me. He said you all would ruin the burro market if you offered such a price when they usually sell for fifty cents. He might have been teasing me a little, but I think their price must be pretty cheap.

The other afternoon I hiked halfway up one of the high hills in front of Wright Peak and lounged back on my coat resting and singing some song in my mind. I was there a long time with my eyes shut. When I jumped up and began singing out loud, there was a great clatter and two deer that had been eating almost at my feet bounded over the rocks and away. Thursday I walked up a hill in front of Pummel Peak, finding chippings and pretty little flowers I've never seen before. This time when I rested I sat with my eyes open and soon a big buck deer strolled around the hill and down in the arroyo not a bit afraid, though he wasn't as near to me as the others had been.

Jackrabbits are shooting about all over the place. They streak out of a bush and go like mad until they are about fifteen feet from me, then they stop and look back. If I don't move, they tuck those long hind legs neatly under them and sit down and watch me. I've never out-stared one yet—they sit and sit and sit as if they had all the time in the world. So finally I have to move on, and they leap up and go too.

We've had three different janitors for the school this year, and they've all quit so the other teacher and I are doing it now and halving the $25 a month janitor salary. AK

APRIL 9, 1953

Dear Mama and All:

Our new school board was elected last Saturday. I didn't hear any results until Monday morning. Gertrude, the other teacher, came in while I was washing dishes. She shooed the children out and shut the door. "Have you heard?" she asked. I was aghast at her expression. I had taken for granted that George would be re-elected president he has done such an excellent job, and I didn't care who else was on the board because he would be the brains of it. Laure, a man without children in school got first place, a woman won second place, and Harold tied George for third place. George has conceded the election to Harold; Harold says he won't take it, so I don't know what is going to happen. The people don't realize how hard George has worked for the school or how much work is involved in being president of the board. Gertrude and I were both shocked.

I've certainly had the social whirl since last Sunday. I went to breakfast at 9 o'clock Easter morning at the Shollys' house. Many people were there— all of Panther Junction and three visiting dignitaries—one from Santa Fe, one from Mammoth Cave, and one from Washington, D.C. We sat about the living room and dining room eating. It was a lovely breakfast—sausage patties in rice, two kinds of coffeecake, fruit, pineapple juice, and coffee. All was beauty and dignity, and I was enjoying myself immensely. Suddenly, across the room from me, Danny (he of the growling lion episode) leaped to his feet and hollered, "Look, Miss Kilgore, look!! Yonder comes the new fireguard!" Everybody roared with laughter. I tried to extricate myself as gracefully as I could, but there wasn't much I could do except I refused to look. I've got to read an etiquette book of some kind. We have two new fireguards for the tourist season, and I've been well-briefed from all sources on both of them. One of them (I've not seen either) lives in a tent at headquarters just across the arroyo from the school.

After breakfast Lon Garrison, park superintendent, had just begun reading aloud the *Esquire* article that has caused such an uproar in Texas, when Rowdy, the Gulliher grandson who went to Korea to escape Alabama, and some of the boys from the ranch came for me to go on the picnic. I dashed home, got the cake I had baked, and away we went. With the Dotts and Gullihers, Steve and me, we had such a crowd we decided to go to Oak Creek Canyon and have our own picnic rather than go to Santa Elena. Oak Creek is an old ranch, very pretty, and we hid Easter eggs for the children and had a sumptuous picnic. We found the remains of a very large Indian camp there, many beautiful chippings, and three metates that the Indians used to grind corn in.

After lunch we went to Dagger Flat to see the daggers, still in bloom and lovely after three weeks of blooming. Then we took the old road to Boquillas to visit Maggie Smith at San Vicente. The day before, a hard rain had fallen in the desert causing a great deal of damage. The men had to rebuild the road as we drove along. I never have seen anything like it, or people like them. We traveled in two pickups—Nealie, Nita Gulliher and Fred Gulliher's sister in the front of one with the back full of boy children; Rowdy and I in the front of the other pickup with Boots and Fred, and a gang of big boys on the back of it. We'd come to where the rain had washed the road out; the men and larger boys would blithely unload, get out the picks and shovels, and fix the road while the women sat about on rocks watching and the children played in the water. When the road was passable, we'd hop in, go a little farther, come to another washout. We'd stop, the men and boys would scout the road ahead; if it were passable through it we'd go. If not, everybody would unload until the men rebuilt the road.

In one place the water had been so high it had eaten away so much of the road the men had to dig off part of a mountain to fill the hole. While we were waiting there most of the younger boys went down to the creek and drank and drank. "Delicious," Steve pronounced. Ugh!

In some places the men had to roll huge boulders out of the road; in one place they had to detour away out in the desert, going over bushes and rocks to get around a deep hole of water blocking the road. I can't remember how many times we had to stop for road repairs. I asked Rowdy how long a pickup lasted out here. He said a good one will last ten months. Everything was most exciting to me, but Boots said it was an old story to them. Everyone acted as if we were at the most fun kind of party, like we were having a lark.

To reach San Vicente and Mrs. Smith's, we had to cross lower Tornillo Creek. I remembered at breakfast that morning George had said six tourist cars had to spend the night on the wrong side of lower Tornillo because the water was raging from the rain. He had sent the two fireguards down with ropes to help the people across—that's why they weren't at the breakfast. When we came to it, the creek was dry but we could see how high the water had been. As we were crossing, Lupe, the Mexican customs official from Boquillas, met us in his car. Everybody stopped in the creek bed to exchange news. At last we got to Mrs. Smith's store. We looked over her animals (she is outside the park now and can have as many as she wants). She has two of the cutest little curly-haired Mexican pigs, peacocks, and a lake full of fish. At dark we started on the long drive back to Nealie's where we prepared supper for the whole gang calmly with no fuss or bother. Meanwhile some of the men had detoured by Woody's fishing camp on the river to pick up a goat body he had bought from a Mexican for barbecuing. They brought it to the house wrapped in canvas. After supper we sat around with Fred, who has been ranching in the Big Bend for thirty-one years, and the other men telling all sorts of wild tales supposedly true. It was certainly an adventurous and enjoyable day.

Monday night I recuperated from Sunday. Tuesday was Reece Sholly's birthday. I went with the superintendent's family to the Sholly house after supper for ice cream, cake, and coffee. I laughed to hear the fantastic stories they all had to tell of their experiences in the park service. Assistant Superintendent Evans told an especially funny story about being awakened at four o'clock one morning with the news that a bear was roaming the hotel lobby at Yellowstone. I was the only non-park service person present so all the tales were new to me.

Last night I had thousands of work to do and had honorable intentions about it when Boots, Nealie, Fred Gulliher and the children came by on the way to Woody's fishing camp. Boots had heard that Woody had caught a fish, so they were all going to see it. I hopped in too. Woody's camp was in a bare place behind a hill safe from the wind, very primitive but typical of a westerner's camp, Boots and Fred said. The stars were sure 'nuff big and bright there. They were hanging right over the Rio Grande, and the soft warm wind was blowing, and all kinds of lovely desert smells were in the air. As we sat around the fire we could hear the burros braying over in Mexico. Every so often we thought we heard a rattlesnake sliding through the cactus. Fred told more tales of the old days. Woody had put the coffee pot on as soon as we got there, as people always do here. As we sipped it, Boots said, "You know, you said you'd never drink Rio Grande water?" I nodded. "Well, you're drinking it now," he said, "and last time you had coffee down here with Woody that was river water you drank." I emptied my cup on a creosote bush, but I'm afraid the damage had already been done. I should have known that coffee flavored with grit and creosote bush couldn't have come from anywhere but the Rio Grande. We came back about ten o'clock bringing Woody's fish, a nice-size cat, wrapped in a tow sack.

Tonight I had thousands of work to do again but Mae and Steve came, bringing supper with them, and we drove out to Dagger Flat to eat. The Flat is still very beautiful, and from the top of a hill we could see daggers blooming away to the horizon and beyond. The blossom stalk is a conglomeration of ivory-white bells that saturate the cool night air with a sweet lemony fragrance, almost like a magnolia blossom smells. The hills, the sky, and the sunset were all most lovely.

Sunday Mae and I are giving a dinner at Mae's house in the Basin for her boss Vince and his wife Tillie who are being transferred. They are both very nice people. I'm to make two black bottom pies. Everybody who has eaten a piece of my black bottom pies likes them very much. Boots especially likes them. I hope to make one for his birthday next Tuesday when Nealie is giving a dinner for both of us in honor of our birthdays. And I hope to take a pie to the Gulliher ranch next time we go. They've been teasing me about Alabama cooking and everything else Alabama, but I've almost convinced Rowdy that he was entirely mistaken about Alabama when he was stationed there.

It's nigh midnight. I must get to bed to rest up for tomorrow. We do folk dancing on Friday mornings in school. It takes strength. Be careful and write. AK

APRIL 11, 1953

Dear Daddy,

I wish I could have been there to help eat that fish you caught. This Rio Grande either has very wise fish in it or else very few of them. The one time I've been fishing in it I saw neither hide nor hair of a fish. I finally saw one of these famous catfish last Wednesday night but it wasn't so imposing. It might have tasted all right though.

Yesterday I was thirty-two years old. Sigh! Where are the years going? The superintendent's wife, Inger, invited me to their house for dinner. We ate in the walled-in backyard surrounded by flowers in bloom. The mountains were gorgeous in the setting sun. The broiled steaks smelled wonderful and tasted wonderfuller. For dessert we had meringues—circles of beaten egg whites slightly browned and filled with ice cream and strawberries. Delicious. Afterwards we sat around a mesquite fire and talked. The chief clerk, Vince, and his family, were guests for dinner too. They are being transferred to Grand Canyon, where the Garrisons came from.

All of Panther Junction came in for dessert, even the new fireguard who has moved into a tent at headquarters and is now my nearest neighbor. He is from Minnesota and seems to be a very nice child (sigh! my age again). Everyone who lives in Panther Junction now is friendly and as nice as can be. The park is a more pleasant and livelier place than it was before Christmas.

You know the picture on the cover of the Baptist Training Union book you sent me? Those flowers look like the giant daggers that grow only in the Big Bend area. Thousands of them grow at Dagger Flat here in the park. They are just now ending the most beautiful blooming season within anyone's memory. The dagger itself grows from fifteen to twenty feet high, then its cluster of creamy blossoms extends upward about five feet. During the three weeks they've been blooming I've gotten to see them four times and each time they've been more beautiful than the last time. On the Monday night that the moon was full I went with the Lundberg family out there. C.K. turned off the station wagon lights, and we drove through those acres and acres of white fragrant blossoms with that full Texas moon shining down on them. I'll never forget that night.

The fly in the ointment here though is the rattlesnake. Those who've lived here a long time say don't get off the trails this time of year because they are lurking everywhere. The Garrisons, the house nearest me, had one on their porch last week. Only Karen, my seventh grader, and her grandmother, who doesn't see well, were at home. The grandmother was sweeping under the porch swing and found a kind of stick she couldn't dislodge no matter how hard she swept it with the broom. Fortunately, she called Karen, who saw it was a rattler and called a neighbor to kill it. It was a traditional brown rattler. We also have green ones and beautiful red racers. Now I guess if I am sensible my after-school walks will have to end because there are no trails back in the Chisos foothills. AK

MAY 3, 1953 - SUNDAY

Dear Mama,

Every day here has been so windy! Last week we had the worst dust storms park people remember. For almost a week the del Carmens, our most beautiful mountains, were invisible. Then one day, as if somebody had lifted a curtain, there they were again.

Dr. and Mrs. Clifton, whom I've known since I was in school at the University of Ala., are coming to the park June 22. I've been considering staying a while after school is out in order to go to some of the places I haven't seen yet. Then I could see the Cliftons when they come, but it would mean I won't be home till the end of June.

The last few weeks (since the Friday before Easter) have been the most wonderful of this whole wonderful and strange year. I've hardly had a minute to spend in my little dust-covered apartment. April 17th all of Panther Junction was gone except Art (the fireguard) and me. I invited Mae and her friend Ray from Odessa, and Art to supper. While we had our black bottom pie and coffee on the school porch and watched the Chisos in the moonlight, the first skunk of this spring strolled around our feet crunching chicken bones.

The next day I lunched at Government Springs and helped Nealie make sandwiches for the dance that night. I was late getting back to their house for the dance because Ray, Mae, Steve, Art, and I had supper at Dugout. Ray fried the chicken that was delicious. Arrived at the Government Springs dance by 9:30 P.M.

Last weekend was a high spot. The Dotts invited me to go with them and some of their friends over on the Pecos River to fish. Two-hundred-twenty miles away from the park. We left Friday afternoon, picked up their friends in Sanderson, got Nealie's mother and father in Dryden, and at eleven that night took off on a dirt road for the huge Chandler Ranch on the Pecos. Three of the men from our party had gone ahead earlier in the day and had prepared camp in a grove of beautiful live oak trees. We made a fire, ate, got out our bedrolls (I had borrowed Mae's sleeping bag), and were in bed by three. Up next morning before the sun rose over the Pecos bluffs. A beautiful clear stream called Independence Creek ran into the Pecos at our campsite. A tasty breakfast—unlimited bacon, eggs, plump biscuits, coffee. We ate bountifully the whole trip—T-bone steaks, cold drinks, everything. We fished in the Pecos all that day in between visiting the various ranches—the old man Chandler has divided the property among his five sons, so each son has his own ranch—seeing their baby Angora goats (dogies, they called them because their mothers had died), dogie lambs, beautiful horses with solid-colored foreparts and spotted hindquarters, and all kinds of dogs (Buster, George, Blondie, etc.). The maternity casualty rate in goats and sheep out on the range must be high because sometimes in a single season one of the Mrs. Chandlers raises thirty orphan goats on bottles and many baby sheep.

Next morning our only luck (besides a moccasin!) was a turtle one of the girls caught and which we used for bait. But in the afternoon late, I stationed myself on a high rock over the edge of the water and caught four fish almost as fast as I could bait my hook (they were little ones but what a thrill—three sun perch and one cat). All day the others had made fun of my pole—a young tree that was so heavy I had to brace it on something in order to hold it. But after my catches they began to think maybe it was a lucky pole since no one else caught anything. One of the redheaded boys swapped poles with me hoping he could catch something, but neither of us caught anything after that. We put out trotlines in the river too but had no luck. Sixteen of us went on this trip. Everybody looked after me and exerted themselves to see that I had a good time.

On Sunday we had people from the various ranches in and out of camp all day, and we were in and out of the ranches all day. I got my comeuppance from one of the Mrs. Chandlers. We had been talking about my home and family in Alabama and how different life is out here. She said, "Aren't you too young to be way out here in this wild country alone?" Indignantly I said, "Why, I've been to New York, and Washington, D.C., and San Diego, and New Jersey . . . ." and I named off everywhere I could remember ever having set foot. When I ran out of places, in the silence, she said meekly, "I've been to San Antone." That deflated me in a hurry!

On Sunday night when we returned to the park we went to the Dotts' house at Government Springs and fried two chickens for supper. The Dotts have three boys. I teach the oldest one, Jack. They treat me like a member of their family. I always enjoy going anywhere with them. Whatever they do and wherever they go, everybody has a good time. They have many friends and always travel in big groups. People go and come in a relaxed and friendly way. Nealie had me over for Boots' birthday dinner April 14th and honored my birthday too. Often on weekends I lunch at their house. They took me to San Vicente with them the other Sunday, brought much food, and we ate it on a big table that's on the school porch. Last Thursday they had people visiting them from Los Alamos, New Mexico. We all went down to Hot Springs along with some people from the concessions and cooked supper. Some of the men fished. How beautiful it was there, with the moon rising over the del Carmens. Far into Mexico we could see a fire burning high on the San Vicente Mountains. The hoot owls were hooting, and we could hear the rush of the muddy Rio Grande as it moved along. (It is about dried up because of the "drouth" of the last three years).

How comical life is in the park. Mae and I invited Pat and Mildred, the Boquillas ranger and his wife, to supper last Friday night at Mae's house in the Basin. Mildred and I were in the kitchen watching Mae fix the green salad. Mildred asked what the greenery was. Mae said it was chard, that Gertrude (the other teacher) had sent it to her. Etta had sent it to Gertrude, Mae said, and Reece had given it to Etta. She thought maybe Reece had grown it in her yard. Mildred laughed and laughed. "No," she said. "I pulled those greens out of my yard at Boquillas and sent them to Reece to begin with."

You never know in whose house you will meet your own possessions. One night I showed Harold a beautiful green rock Bob Gibbs had given me. Harold recognized it as one he had found in New Mexico and had given to Bob.

When I am in the Basin on a Saturday and need a ride to Panther Junction, I catch the Panther Junction Express, Mac Waters' jeep. Mac is the one who keeps the generators functioning and always makes a run between the two settlements on Saturday morning.

I told you all how Danny embarrassed me at Reece's Easter breakfast by shrieking for me to look quick, there was the new fireguard. If I had known how nice he was I would certainly have craned my neck to look. I didn't meet him until my birthday dinner with the Garrisons when he came over for dessert and coffee. I thought at that time if I were eighteen I'd certainly wave my eye-lashes at him. His name is Arthur, he is twenty-eight, the son of a St. Paul medical doctor, intelligent, nice looking, a Lutheran who doesn't drink or smoke. He is here for the same reason I am—to find out about the place. Every day he comes across the arroyo to see me. When I was at Mae's on a Sunday night when she was having other guests, she also invited him, but he had to cancel at the last minute because of a fire down on the river. He has been over twice today and is bringing steak for our supper tonight. Yesterday after he got off from work he came and mopped the whole school. He has rigged up his radio for me with an aerial. Everybody has fallen for him, especially the children, even Steve.

One night Art brought up a bottle of milk that had soured. (He has no refrigerator in his tent.) He thought I might use it in cooking which I do a lot of. I insisted he take a bottle of sweet milk in place of the sour so he would have something to drink. (It was Monday and he would have no more milk until the following Sunday). Only we two were involved, and I do not know how anyone else knew about it, but at Fire School, which all park men are attending now, the men were being fined for foolish and funny reasons to make money for their coffee breaks. Harold fined Art a quarter for "bringing sour milk to the teacher's house and taking sweet milk away."

One day Art brought to school a collection of mats, baskets, and sandals woven by Indians six hundred to two thousand years ago. They were found in a cave near the park. The children and I enjoyed seeing them and hearing about them.

On April 28 I was invited for an enchilada supper at Government Springs and went dancing with the Dotts and their friends to Polk Hinson's store at Study Butte till one in the morning. What sad music the Mexican bands play! It seems to fit this vast, lonely, deadly country.

After lunch Friday, May 1st, all the school went out to Tornillo Flat to see a Fire School demonstration. The men planned to start a fire in the old Starr ranch house and show how easily a fire could be put out if it is caught in time. But within one minute after the fire started it was too much out of control to be extinguished—the house was so dry it burned in a short time.

Today Mae, Steve, and Art came to early supper so we could drive to K Bar ranch and see the Lundberg children's cactus blossoms. But the weather was so cold all blossoms had closed! Take care. Write. AK

MAY 24, 1953

Dear Mary Alice,

The weather is very hot now and dry; the dust settles on everything every day. The Rio Grande is rapidly evaporating. From this schoolhouse there isn't a tree in sight except some very young ones that have been set out in the yards of the five houses across the arroyo.

Nealie and Boots had Art and me over to Government Springs for supper Friday night. Nealie cooked beet tops the way Mama fixes turnip greens. They were good, seeing as how it's been so long since I've had greens, but not as tasty as mustard and turnip greens. Nealie cooks chard a lot too, something else we never had at home.

It is hard for me to remember those two years of teaching in Alabama. It seems to me now that I did nothing but work then, hard work, while here there is danger of the social life dominating the work completely. However, my students have completed all their books, and I feel I have done a good job teaching them.

Monday night two weeks ago the board of trustees offered me this job again for next year and I accepted. I felt I would like to give it one more year, now that I know the children and have become somewhat adjusted to this way of life. Then too it would be hard to face a new place so soon after tackling this one.

I've saved about seven hundred dollars this year. I'm yearning to come home.

The Carrolls, from the ranch I visited that weekend, are in Byhalia, Miss. now. Mrs. Carroll writes that they've had so much rain there she longs for this Texas sunshine. I can't imagine rain like that. We have not had a genuine rain since I've been here, except during Christmas vacation when I was away.

May 5th Art went with the Garrisons and a party of people to Ojinaga. Mexico, for the Fiesta. I went with Boots and Nealie to the Gulliher ranch. Fred claims he's found just the man for me—he has two oil wells, "but one of them ain't a'pumpin'."

The Dotts resolved to remain at home for that weekend, so they invited me to come spend the night. Theirs is an old ranch house from the days long before Big Bend became a national park. A hoot owl sat on the chimney all night and hooted, but that only added to the atmosphere. We had waffles for breakfast. Boots and I fixed supper on Sunday, and Art came over to join us. We laughed about a dish Woody fixes at his fishing camp—"fried turtle a la Woody."

The next night Steve and Mae came by the school on their way into the park from Odessa. They and Art had supper with me. On Tuesday, Art's off day, he came right after school was out and we hiked the Lost Mine trail, near the Basin. We went all the way to the top (two-and-a-fourth miles), stopping to look at everything—bird, beast, fish, or plant—that interested us. The view from the top is a thing of wonder. We stayed up to watch the sun set and then came down. Lions have been seen frequently on this trail in the last few weeks so we kept a special lookout for them, though we saw not a sign of one.

The lions are showing themselves all over the park now more than usual. Not long ago a man and woman from Dallas were on Lost Mine trail when a lion strolled up to them and sank its teeth in the man's trouser leg. The couple stood still, and soon the lion walked away. The park people claim the lions are only curious.

The barbecuing committee of the Casa Grande Club hung up three sheep in the Basin last week to be barbecued next day. A lion spent the night roaring and clawing at a sheep body trying to get it down to eat. Because of these incidents, and rattlesnakes, and lack of time, I don't go walking any more by myself.

It seems that my main association lately is with Art. He comes up every night, and if we aren't invited out to supper, we eat here, with him furnishing the T-bone steaks and ice cream. We eat with the Dotts often, and last week while some Jehovah's Witness workers visited Mae we ate with them several times, picnicking or at Mae's house.

Last Saturday Etta invited me to Hot Springs with her and Patty (my fourth grader). Etta's husband, Pete, was away, and we were to keep the store for him. We were having an enjoyable time talking with the tourists and playing along the river when Art came by and invited me to go to Lower Hot Springs and Boquillas Canyon with him. Another ranger, Bob, and his wife Lynn were with him but in a separate truck. I would not have gone as I felt I was Etta's guest first, but she insisted, so Art and I went to clean the campgrounds at Lower Hot Springs (pick up glass, tin cans, cigarette butts, etc.) while Bob and Lynne went to clean the Boquillas campground.

We found Nealie's brother, Woody, and his Uncle Amos camping and fishing at Lower Hot Springs. They had been there for seven days and caught nothing! Just as Art and I were parting with them, here came Boots, Nealie, and the boys to eat dinner with Woody and Uncle Amos. We added the food Art had brought for our lunch to their cake and potato salad, and Woody and Uncle Amos contributed corn pone and frijoles, making a delicious meal that we ate sitting around on the ground beside the river.

Art and I then went to Boquillas Canyon to look for Bob and Lynne, but they were nowhere about. How hot and dry and thirsty we were. (Art's canteen was in Bob's truck.) We stopped in at the Boquillas ranger station where Pat and Mildred used to live (they are at Persimmon Gap now at the park entrance). The house is vacant so we roamed through it. Very attractive, Spanish style, with a courtyard in front surrounded by a high wall, and black marble floors on different levels. For a time we sat on the wall watching the Rio Grande struggle by below. We also saw, from a distance, the Dotts plowing through the river to Boquillas, the village in Mexico. We could see the mill in the village where the ore is crushed after it is brought from the mines deep in Mexico before it is trucked through the park to the railroad at Marathon.

The day was getting along toward five when we went wading in the river to cool off a bit and with the hope of finding water to drink. Down the river apiece we saw a clear spring pouring out of the Mexican side. We waded over and drank and drank—the water was warm but good.

We bounced home by way of Hot Springs where we found Pete had returned with a load of mattresses and things he had bought to furnish his tourist cabins. Art helped him unload, and then we drove to Panther Junction. We went to our respective abodes for baths, then took Art's T-bone steaks and hied ourselves to Dugout for supper—the end to a lovely day.

The next night we ate supper at Mae's with her Kingdom Hall workers. On Monday we stayed with Danny and Debbie Sholly at their house while George and Reece went to an official dinner at the Garrisons' house. (George has been disabled by a lecheguilla thorn that speared him in the knee.) On Tuesday night we went to the barbecue honoring the visiting officials. The sheep meat was delicious even though it had been pawed by the lion. The children acted rather silly—they are crazy about Art, which only makes them act sillier. He and I went to the club kitchen for a drink of water; the children waited a few minutes, then rushed in as one body to "catch us," they thought. You should have seen their faces fall when they found us sitting across the room from each other, and Art really drinking a glass of water.

The Girl Scouts had their last meeting of the year on Wednesday, a cook-out. Afterwards Art and I carried the Grapevine Hills Scouts home. Art had Pinedo, the girls' uncle, cut his hair while the children took me on a guided tour of their settlement, which is an old ranch (now within the park). Three Mexican families who work for the park live there.

On our way home we stopped to visit with Boots, Nealie, and the boys, and they invited us to a fried catfish supper Friday night. Then we drove back to the school for ice cream. On Thursday night we had another steak-and-ice-cream dinner, at my house this time. On Friday night we ate catfish with the Dotts and went to the Gulliher ranch with them. Yesterday Art came up for lunch and for supper we ate more steak and ice cream. I baked cookies this morning, and the Dotts came for a while. Then Steve arrived to spend the day. When Art came across the arroyo for lunch, Steve reprimanded him for holding my hand in public the night we went to explore the Oak Creek Canyon ranch house and spring. "It's all over Big Bend that you held the teacher's hand," he said.

Art is coming up for supper tonight. I am wondering when this close association is going to get monotonous to us—no sign yet. He is very nice, but we haven't serious intentions, I don't think. I don't believe I'd ever consider marrying anybody. I enjoy my freedom too much—but he is certainly fun to be with.

Seven more days of school! The closing date has been set back to June 2nd. I am bringing Nealie's delicious chocolate potato cake recipe back to Alabama with me. AK

JUNE 16, 1953

Dear Mary Alice,

We've closed school after struggling through our program for the parents, which was the most casual program I ever saw presented. My register still isn't ready to turn in—it is a mess, and I dread tackling it again but finished it must be.

It is sure 'nuff hot here. The tourists straggle in to headquarters looking for a cool place. Art sends them to Boquillas Canyon or Santa Elena Canyon where it is cool, but they have to struggle through the torrid, dry desert, past the evaporated Rio Grande in order to get to either place. The heat doesn't bother me—it is dry heat, and usually a breeze blows through the school, so I don't suffer.

I enjoyed the clippings and cartoons you all sent. I'm going to be so behind in world news I'll never catch up. *Newsweek* is still coming but there is no time to sit down and read it.

My land! I heard a little noise and looked down, and there came a lizard sliding under the door. The other night Art and I were eating supper with the same door open, and a monstrous tarantula walked in. Any day I expect to see a lion strolling among the desks. I keep the outside door open to make the building cooler, so the varmints are taking advantage of it.

Mrs. Garrison, the park superintendent's wife, sent a vase of gladiolas for school closing. They are even more beautiful than usual when you see them in this arid land. At the children's benefit program one of the men auctioned off a vase of them one at a time for one dollar to two-fifty each.

The ranchers here are in despair because of the drouth. Springs that have never been known to dry up are completely gone. The river is a smelly muddy trickle. The last rains that came anywhere near here were the 24th and 26th of May. Art and Steve had supper here the 24th (Art furnishing the steak), but we ate supper piecemeal as the lightning was striking sotol plants all over the Dead Horse Mountains and starting fires. George (chief ranger) would come to tell Art where he was going to investigate for fire. Art would go to radio the Basin to be on the alert, Mr. Giles would come for Art to come to the radio, and finally word did come for Art to take the fire truck on the Glen Springs road near Nugent Peak. Steve was crushed because he couldn't go on the truck but Mae was to come by for him on her way in from Alpine and it was so late I was afraid he might miss her. Sometimes the men have to stay out all night or longer on those fires.

The following Tuesday rain fell back in the Rosillos Mountains and on Tornillo Flat between Panther Junction and Marathon. Art was off that day, and as soon as school was out we started for Alpine to buy the accessories for his ranger uniform (he is moving up from fireguard!). Every creek we went through was rising, but we didn't worry much as we thought they would be down again before we got back. I couldn't help but think what a juicy morsel for the gossip circle of the Basin if Tornillo would be impassable on our way back, and we had to spend the night on the wrong bank waiting for it to go down. Between Marathon and Alpine we drove through a deluge, and though it was closing time for the stores by the time we finally got to town, they were most gracious and took all the time necessary to show us what we wanted to see. Shopping in Alpine is a social occasion anyway—introductions, discussions of the weather and what's going on in the park are always in order.

That trip to Alpine was one of the most enjoyable evenings I've ever spent—nothing happened the whole evening to detract from it. After we had finished shopping and running errands for park people, we had dinner at a very nice place across from the college; then we went to a movie—Crosby and Hope in *The Road to Bali*. On the way home none of the creeks were running except Tornillo, which was still rushing away but much lower than when we had crossed it earlier. But while we were in town it had risen so high some of the park people had come out to watch it run. At midnight when we crossed there was nobody else out except us and the jackrabbits.

I've been to many interesting places with Art—one was to San Vicente on the river to see Maggie Smith, the border character I've written you all about before. On the way there we stopped to look over anything that caught our eye, and at Mrs. Smith's we had an interesting talk and saw her Mexican pigs, white turkeys, and peacocks. The Mexicans had just brought a load of candelilla wax (remember that plant I brought home Christmas?) across the river. We saw it stacked on Mrs. Smith's back porch. It is illegal to sell or make the wax in the park and illegal for Mexicans to sell it in our country anywhere because their government wants to buy it from them at a low price. But Mrs. Smith lives just on the edge of the park so the officials can't do anything to her, and I guess the Mexican gov't doesn't know what she's doing. While we were there the Dotts came along, and we added more food from Mrs. Smith's store to what Art and I had with us, and all of us went to Hot Springs to cook supper.

One night at the school as we were eating supper, Mr. Evans, the assistant superintendent, came for Art to go investigate a fire at Lower Hot Springs. Art uses George's gov't car while George is away, so we hopped in it and had a nice thirty-mile drive to the river in the cool of the evening. Some men from Fort Stockton were camping there under the arbor where we had eaten lunch with the Dotts the day I went to work with Art. While all the men had been on the river fishing, they heard an explosion at their camp. They reached the arbor in time to save only their bedding and a small icebox. The fire was still burning when we arrived.

On our way back to Panther Junction we stopped by Hot Springs to visit Pete Koch. He had just attended a rain dance in Mexico with Maggie Smith. He told us about it as we sat in a dim light on his patio, so near the river we could hear it murmuring past. He had a gorgeous chunk of clear green rock with a gold nugget in its heart that he bought from a Mexican for $5.00.

One afternoon we went to Study Butte, a deserted quicksilver mining town outside the park. We browsed around in Polk Hinson's store there—he offered me a job working for him this summer—then we started for Terlingua. On the way we stopped at the one filling station for gas and saw Frank, one of my sixth graders, out in the corral. He took us on a tour of the place and then went to Terlingua with us. We explored the old hotel, the abandoned mine and furnace, the graveyard, and the school, all deserted now. We looked through the window of the post office to see letters dumped in the floor of a back room. I've heard that some years ago a stamp collector from the park went into the post office and found many valuable stamps on the letters.

Now that school is out I use the schoolroom as a dining room when guests come. The big school table is our dining table, and we have a spacious cool place for eating, with a splendid view. One Sunday night Mae, Steve, Art, and Andy (who now lives with Art in the tent), and I ate in there. I cooked most of the meal, and it was good too. Art bought most of it, and Andy brought records so we had a concert too.

The day after that dinner I kept the four Lundberg children (two sets of twins) while their parents made an emergency trip to town from 8 A.M. to 9:30 P.M. We had such a good time. We collected Indian chippings and arrowheads from the foothills near the school, and they helped me with the housework. Andy was working on the fire hose box here at school, and they enjoyed talking to him. For lunch we had the four children, Art, Mae, Andy, and myself. We disposed of all the leftovers from the night before plus the food Ruth and C.K. had brought when they delivered the children. After Art got off from work he took us for a ride out on the Marathon road to visit those graves with the weathered wooden crosses. For supper we decided to have sandwiches on the school porch and Art's ice cream for dessert. The children guzzled that ice cream. Then we told stories that scared us so bad we all ended up on top of the table because we heard snuffling sounds in the darkness around us. As the night grew late, Art and I decided we should take the twins home to K Bar and put them to bed. Before we could load ourselves in the car, however, Ruth and C.K. drove up. They brought me a handsome Max Factor compact as a thank-you gift.

I often keep children when parents have to leave the park—Jack and Millard Ray spent the day with me when Boots and Nealie had to go to the dentist unexpectedly. I stayed with Debbie Sholly one evening recently, and another day Art brought Danny over to stay with me, but I wasn't home so he had to take him to Grandma Larsen at the Garrisons' house. Fortunately, I like all the children and we get along well.

The Lundbergs had Art and me to dinner Friday night. Before we ate the children took us strawberry hunting—the fruit of the strawberry cactus tastes as delicious as strawberries. K Bar is an old ranch house. The kitchen walls and ceilings have bullet holes in them from explosive incidents of the past. AK

JUNE 16, 1953

Dear Mama,

Art often brings interesting tourists to the schoolhouse to meet me. Two of the most attractive have been Col. Raborg and his wife Liz from Laredo. Col. Raborg came through the Big Bend in 1916 with Gen. Pershing's cavalry after the Glen Springs raid by Pancho Villa's men. The sun was so scorching hot on men and horses they rode at night and rested in daytime, he said. They ate supper with us—I had barbecued chicken, biscuits, ice cream, etc. We took them to the Boquillas ranger station to show them the house and the canyon. We sat a while in the canyon under the starlight talking. Col. Raborg said that as he travels about this country and compares experiences with other travelers, some of them say, "Have you been to Calcutta?" "Have you seen the Taj Mahal by moonlight?" and name other sights they sigh for. But he answers, "No, but have you been to Boquillas?" We came by Hot Springs to see Pete who gave us two Rio Grande catfish. Saw a raccoon on the way back to Panther Junction.

I've gotten reservations to look through the telescope up in the Davis Mountains the last Wednesday night in this month. Only one night in a month do they let the public look through it, and then the visitor list is limited to two hundred. It is the third largest reflector telescope in the world, McDonald Observatory. You remember when we took the children there before Christmas we didn't get to see through it because of the weather (windy, icy, and snowing). Art and I plan to drive up to the Davis Mtns with the Cliftons and stay overnight as everybody in the park will be aware that we are well chaperoned. The Cliftons already have reservations at the showplace for tourists to stay, The Indian Lodge, for themselves, so I know we can shuffle ourselves about and Mr. Clifton and Art can stay together.

Art and I spent an enjoyable evening with Boots and Nealie on Sunday. We had barbecued steaks in the shady yard (not tree shade, but house shade). We sat talking until after dark. Jack, my fifth-grader, jumped on his bicycle and sped away from where we were sitting. About ten feet from us, in the dark, he leaped off his bicycle shrieking, "Rattlesnake, Daddy! Rattlesnake!" Sure enough it was. Jack had run over it, and though he couldn't see, he recognized the rattle. Boots killed it because it was too close to a habitation. It was the first rattlesnake I've seen in Big Bend, but they tell me there are oodles of them here.

A tourist fell off Vernon Bailey Peak in the Basin a couple of Saturdays ago. He lay all night with broken legs, broken nose, and gashes all over him. Art said there was a bloody trail where he had dragged himself trying to summon help. His partner was higher up on the peak unable to get down. Fortunately, the power plant in the Basin failed on Sunday morning so there was quiet. When Mac Waters went to work on the motor at eight o'clock he heard their faint cries for help and notified the rangers. Art and Harold did the rescue work. Art was the first one to reach the uninjured man. He said he never saw anyone so glad to see him. The man wrung Art's hand and could hardly express himself. When they finally got down, Art's clothes were in rags and he was all scratched up. Mickey and Byrum Waller in the Basin took him home with them for a shower and Byrum lent him a set of his clothes to wear back to Panther Junction. As soon as Art returned he came to my house and collapsed on the rug. I didn't realize how tired he was, and when Mae, Ray, and Steve came for us to eat with them down at Hot Springs I twisted his arm and made him go. I was sorry afterward.

Mary Alice asked what had happened to Harold. He is still here, and I see him once in a while though he has actually been to see me only one time since Art came, and that was during school time. Twice he has invited me on a picnic but I haven't gone because I didn't like his manners on the last picnic I went on with him. Steve, who sees him often, told me last Sunday that Harold wanted to ask me to go swimming with him at Balmorhea, a beautiful pool quite a long way from here in the Davis Mountains. I told Steve I didn't want him passing on to me anything Harold had to say about me because I don't like people who won't speak for themselves. I wouldn't have gone anyway now.

Today Art is working at the Persimmon Gap Ranger Station, twenty-five miles away from Panther Junction, and he wasn't coming to lunch, so I didn't intend to take time out from work to eat by myself. But Harold was at headquarters without lunch (he lives in the Basin) so he persuaded Mae to come over here with him to see if I'd give him a sandwich. We had a pleasant lunch together, and they lingered way past their time for going. They were talking about what a good lunch it was and Mae was teasing Harold about letting me escape him, when Harold looked down at his plate and said, "I took her on a picnic once, and when I brought her home she told me to go and not come back." Mae said, "Well, I sure have wondered what happened to you two." It didn't happen as bluntly as that or as melodramatically, but it amounted to the same thing. There are many things about Harold that are admirable, and one of them is that he will spare nothing to help a person out. He outdoes himself to help the tourists, to inform them, and to take them about. On his own time he shows his slides to groups of them. But personally he is not an admirable person, at least not to me.

The Shollys are away now, and Panther Junction folks are tending their yard for them. Art and I spent one afternoon down there, I spectating, and Art doing the work, mowing and watering. When he finished he took me to tour his tent and see his shower he's so proud of—a metal drum on a high platform, filled with water warmed by the sun.

The watering pan in my yard stays busy now. Birds have it during the day, and after the sun goes down, there is a continuous procession of mammals— foxes of all sizes, skunks, deer, coyotes, and ringtails. Though it is sometimes too dark to see, I can hear the stealthy movements. The Bledsoes, who live next to the Shollys, told us they sometimes watch a panther standing on the rock wall that encloses the Garrisons' garden. It is silhouetted against the house lights and seems to be observing what goes on in the Garrison yard. Spied on by a panther! Wouldn't that be thrilling? AK

JULY 6, 1953 - MONDAY NIGHT - HOUSTON, TEXAS

Dear Daddy,

I surely had a lovely time before leaving Big Bend. On Thursday afternoon Art and I went hiking in the Grapevine Hills Canyon, one of the most striking places in the park. We were looking for that balanced rock where Harold made my picture that time, but we never found it. We saw a panther track as big as my hand, though, and deer were all around us. It is a beautiful and strange place. That night we went to dinner at Mae's and had our usual enjoyable time.

My reservation had come on Wednesday to leave Friday at 8:15 P.M. on the Sunset Limited. Early Friday morning Art drove to the school, we put my bags in the car, and started out on a wonderful day. On the way to Marathon we saw a red racer, a rosy-red snake I had heard a lot about but had never seen. Of course, we stopped to look it over. We did errands and paid bills in Marathon and Alpine, then went to Marfa and explored a pretty little park there full of flowers, trees, and greenery. We enjoyed walking through it, as everything in our park is so burned up from lack of water. Then we went to Presidio, Texas, down on the river, and crossed to Ojinaga, Mexico, by way of a rickety privately owned toll bridge. The town was fascinating, very different from Boquillas, Mexico, across the river from our park. We sat in the town square on benches made of granite (each one inscribed with a name and date like a memorial) and watched the town life pass by. They have an attractive modern school that we toured, and we took our time strolling around the town. We poked about in the little stores (bought a record of a sad song called, "Adios, Margarita") and visited the church. Powerful odors hovered in the streets—apparently the town has no sewers. It was all fascinating to me.

We drove back to Marfa for supper—steaks at the Paisano Hotel, which is famous for its food. Most delicious. We planned to be back in Alpine by 8:15 P.M. (twenty-six miles away) so I could pick up my ticket and reservation for the Limited. While we were waiting for dessert I decided I would call the Marfa station and see how the Limited was running—probably late, I was sure. I explained at the hotel desk why I wanted a phone and the girl said, "That's the Limited in the station now." No dessert for us! By the time we passed the Marfa station the train had already pulled out for Alpine. Away we went, finally outstripping it when it had to slow down for a hill. When I went in to claim my ticket at Alpine the train came around the bend blowing its whistle. That was too close. AK

JULY 16, 1953 - HOUSTON, TEXAS

Dear Mary Alice,

I don't think I ever mentioned the Cliftons' visit to Big Bend. They arrived a day late because their car broke down in the Pecos River Canyon near the bridge. They finally limped into Sanderson to spend the night they were supposed to arrive in Big Bend. It wasn't till 2 P.M. the next day that they drove into the park. That meant they had only that afternoon and night before leaving early the next morning to keep to their schedule. I've been in the park ten months and I've not seen nearly all the places I want to see, so it was frustrating to me that they had so little time there.

That night Art and I were to meet them for dinner at the Indian Lodge in the Davis Mountains. To expedite our plans, I went to work with Art out to the Persimmon Gap ranger station and at noon we left for our rendezvous one-hundred-forty miles away. The Davis Mountains are more gently beautiful than the park, and the Indian Lodge is lovely. It is run by the Texas Highway Department and is set in the mountains with no other buildings in sight as far as you can see. Behind the lodge is a patio with a wishing well, ivy climbing the wall, and many varieties of cacti with a scattering of animal skulls. The lobby has hewn ceiling beams and polished cedar furniture. We sat on the spacious front gallery and looked at the beautiful scenery. I loved it.

After dinner the Cliftons, Art, and I went in Art's car to the Mt. Locke Observatory as that was the night we were to look through the telescope. My second try, and lo, the sky was too cloudy! We were disappointed, but an astronomer gave us an interesting lecture.

I stayed at the lodge that night. Art found a comfortable place in the park that surrounds the lodge and slept in his sleeping bag. We met for a good breakfast next morning in the lodge dining room. Then we did some sight seeing with the Cliftons. We left them touring old Fort Davis, which we had already seen, and went on to Balmorhea, a large outdoor swimming pool beyond Ft. Davis. While we were there the Cliftons dropped by just for a minute on their way to Carlsbad. Art and I lunched at Balmorhea and decided we would go back to the park by way of the scenic loop to see a pile of rocks where Kit Carson had signed his name. We stopped at three places to ask directions but nobody could tell us where it was.

On the long drive home we stopped one time for supper and bought a watermelon to take back with us. We arrived in the park at midnight. It seemed we had been away for ages. I had a lovely time. See you within a week.
Aileen

PART TWO

A Second Year
September 1953 — May 1954

SEPTEMBER 13, 1953 - PANTHER JUNCTION

Dear Mary Alice,

This has been a wonderful week all the way round. How different it was this year coming back to children I knew and a place I was already used to. Mae and Steve picked me up in Alpine last Sunday afternoon. On the way to the park we stopped at a man's rock shop. He collects agates around the country-side, cuts and polishes them, and makes them into beautiful jewelry. He had one brooch that looked like a landscape with trees reflected in a lake—$300! Mae and Steve ate supper with me and left about ten. It was good to get in my little house again.

The children were all ready for school and have pitched right in to work. I have only seven so far but will probably end up with eight. I've worked hard every night planning their lessons and schedules, but it pays off because our days go so smoothly. What a day was yesterday—I went to the Gulliher ranch with the Dotts. We left before 9:00 A.M.. and got back about 5:30 P.M. The men at the ranch were driving 588 head of sheep about ten miles from one pasture to another. Jack, Millard Ray, Boots, and I went out in the pickup to carry lunch to the herders and see the sheep go. Poor things—how they were panting, their sides heaving. Every time they came to a little shade they would stop in it and nibble a bite. Three miles from Tornillo Creek Grandpa Gulliher let me have his horse, and I herded in his place the rest of the way. The horse was insulted—he turned his head and looked me over with disdain—and refused to go until Fred got a switch for me. Then I struck the beast a blow—harder than I meant to—and he jumped straight up in the air and I did too—I was so startled. Fred almost fell off his horse laughing. How sorry I felt for those poor sheep. When they smelled the waterhole in the creek bed they began to bleat and run. I thought they would surely be sick they drank so much. I reached the creek safely on Grandpa G's horse but my legs didn't work very well when I dismounted.

As most of the creek bed was dry we drove the pickup down the creek bed spreading feed pellets for the sheep. Boots said the sheep were very fat (they just looked ugly to me) as Fred has had them on a planted pasture rather than the desert pasture.

We came home sooner than we wanted to because the Garrisons were giving a barbecue for an organization of businessmen called the "Highway 90 Club," and they had invited me. Much as I wanted to stay at the ranch I sho' didn't want to miss the barbecue. So by 6:30 P.M. I had on my pink dress and was across the arroyo.

Sixty-five to seventy business people came, some from Mexico. They are interested in exploring ways to lure tourists to this part of the country. The Garrisons' yard is full of blooms and enclosed by a high wall (the one the panther walks on). We sat on mats scattered on the lawn during supper, which was delicious goat, beef, salad, a cowboy dish they call in public "son-of-a-gun stew" but in private something unprintable, they say, and hot bread and apple pie. Very good. I already knew some of the people, but I met many more, all very pleasant. Pete Koch showed a beautiful film he has made about the park. He is certainly a marvelous photographer. The evening was very enjoyable.

Today Willie, the grocery man, has come, and I've put everything away. So far I've carried out my resolution to be more economical with food. I eat plenty but waste nothing. The poor skunks haven't gotten much since I came back. After they investigate the food place they come on the patio and look in the door as if to say, "Can't you do better than that?" I must work on my schoolbooks. Take care. AK

Dear Art,

Your letter came in last Friday's mail. I'm glad you got home to St. Paul safely. What a long drive you had from Alabama, but how happy I was you came by my home! And now you have another long drive to your new assignment in Virginia. Go carefully.

This week I've been back has been a good one. Mae and Steve met me. Steve was excited about picking cotton (two dollars a hundred pounds) and he plans to go up near Ft. Stockton this weekend to hire himself out as a cotton picker.

I've discovered I have mice. One of them is so cute and fat and grey. He lives behind the chest of drawers, and every night I see him go under the door into the schoolroom. This morning Willie brought me a mousetrap, and I've just set it so, poor thing, he hasn't long to run about.

The children were eager for school to begin, and they've behaved well. We've all worked hard. The first day of school none of the students from Grapevine Hills appeared. The second day, Eligio and Rozmo came. The third day Eligio brought me a note from Petra saying she and Little Mary wanted to come to school but her daddy wouldn't let them. I don't understand at all, but it seems that Pinedo is still a threat to the girls in some way even though his wife is in Marathon now expecting a baby. If you were here we'd go to the Grapevine Hills to investigate. Eligio told Gertrude his daddy was going to kill Pinedo, etc. Don't you miss the drama of the Big Bend country?

Harris, the Bledsoe child, started to school this year, and he's having a hard time adjusting. During the day we hear all kinds of odd noises coming from Gertrude's classroom on the other side of the curtain. One afternoon I heard Gertrude say, "Well, Harris, where are you going?" and Harris said, "I'm going home. I'm tired." Gertrude was a little surprised, I think, but she persuaded him to stay a while longer. He came in one afternoon and told Gertrude that Millard Ray was on the school grounds chewing tobacco. Before Gertrude could get outside to see, Harris had gone back and gotten such a big chew from Millard the juice was running out both corners of his mouth. Millard Ray said his grandpa (Nealie's father) gave him a whole plug of tobacco.

The animals are gradually coming back for water and food. The skunks have been here every night, and deer show up every afternoon, four or five of them together, but I saw my first fox come tonight at supper. Watermelons are growing around the watering place from the watermelons we ate while you were here, and a cantaloupe vine is blooming. I was amazed to see them. There is a buck deer out there now though—he'll probably eat them.

I saw Pine Canyon last night but not in person as you did. It looked every bit as beautiful as you said it is. Pete showed one of his movies at a barbecue in the Garrison yard, in honor of the "Highway 90 Club," which is made up of businessmen along H'wy 90. Some Mexican businessmen were there from Villa Acuna. Pete's film was about two hours long, but not nearly long enough, I thought. In one scene he had his camera look straight up the trunk of one of the pine trees—Ponderosa, did you say?—and he showed a waterfall at one end of the canyon which is there during the rainy season, he said. Legend says there are eighteen burro-loads of silver at the foot of the falls. Shall we go look for them?

Glenn Burgess was there last night. Do you remember that trip into Mexico he told us he wanted to make this summer? He made it, he said. They climbed to the top of the del Carmens, then four thousand feet higher on the Fronteresias. He said there is a sheer drop of several thousand feet beyond El Sentinel, the highest peak of the Fronteresias, into a canyon as beautiful as Grand Canyon. They were several hundred feet from the top of the Fronteresias when they came down.

I hope I make you homesick for Big Bend. Is that possible? It is certainly hard for me to get used to life here without you. You are like the ghost of the Chisos—everywhere I turn there is something remindful of you. Almost every night this week I've had supper with Brahms—I put the phonograph in your place and have his Concerto #2 in B Flat Major—one of my favorites. I've had time for only one walk since I came back. I went where I used to go before you came, to a hill away up high where the wind always blows, and there is a comfortable rock for sitting and a nice one for leaning back. I used to take my supper there sometimes and watch for lions while I ate. I never had any luck, as you know, but this year I'm still hoping.

Those squished places in this letter are bug bodies. Aileen

Dear Mama,

I've not had a chance to be lonely I've been working so hard. I am doing the janitor work of the school now, hoping to work out my rent. That would be the same as earning $30 each month. It's getting old already, but I keep plugging away with the rent in mind. I've just scrubbed out both the boys' and girls' bathrooms and swept and dusted both schoolrooms—I'm weary.

It is so beautiful here, especially in the mornings and at sunset. We've been having many clouds early and late so that makes the sky more spectacular. The del Carmens, that beautiful striped mountain range in Mexico, is luminous long after sunset. Park officials are working hard on the international park they hope to create on both sides of the border with the help of Mexico.

I'll mail this in Marathon tomorrow as I'm going in with Nealie while Boots is working on the road to the Gulliher ranch. Sunday, if I finish my work, I'm to go to Hot Springs with Mae and Steve for lunch and to make pictures. Aileen

SEPTEMBER 27, 1953
TO ARTHUR HENDERSON, RANGER, BLUE RIDGE PARKWAY,
BUENA VISTA, VIRGINIA

Dear Art,

I am happy that all is going so well with you. I looked for your town on the map. How do they pronounce it there—Big Bend Spanish or English?

When I was at Headquarters for mail the other afternoon I saw the slides George made when he and Lon Garrison flew over the del Carmens. They were beautiful—very rugged with much thick, big timber. Some of the slides showed a sawmill that is working there now. In one section it looked as if every other tree was dead. Drouth, George said. I hear rumors that the candelilla wax situation is more serious than ever. George said under no circumstances would he recommend that anyone travel the river road to Presidio. At Castolon two Mexicans have been killed (by Mexicans) because of candelilla. I wonder who receives it on the U.S. side now that Maggie is gone from San Vicente.

I've a pet of my own now. Not one of Willie's handsome kittens that I wanted (offspring of that gorgeous white cat that lives in Willie's store, remember?) but a bird, which I thought I'd never want. Ruth and C.K. asked me to keep Tweetie, their old parakeet, to see if their younger one would get along all right alone. If so they wanted me to have Tweetie because the two birds together drove C.K. out of his wits. I took the bird to accommodate them but now I enjoy her. I leave her out of the cage all day. Then when she is ready for bed she goes in on her little roost, and I close the door and cover her. In the late afternoons she positions herself where she can watch out the window for the fox. When he comes she sits quietly, hardly breathing, seeing every move he makes. Or I think that's what she's doing.

Life goes on here in the same old way. Petra and Little Mary are in school at last after their father, Raphael, told George he couldn't let them ride to school with Pinedo. The park gave Raphael a truck so all the children from Grapevine commute with him now.

Steve, Danny, and I hiked to Panther Springs last Sunday afternoon. I was certain we'd see a panther, and the farther we went the more certain I was. As soon as we got in the canyon we found panther tracks, and at one place we found leg bones of a deer that was so recently eaten it was still moist. No luck, though. Danny and Steve quarreled all the way there and back. Any animals had plenty of time to get out of our way before we came in sight. The canyon was interesting though, and I thought very beautiful up at the springs, especially the view of Wright Peak.

Boots and Nealie gave an old-time western dance at their house Friday night. The whole countryside was there (mostly old-timers and ranch people), and it lasted till nearly dawn. Each woman took a special dish and eating went on all night. Two "cowboys" from Marathon played the "git-tars" and sang. It was something to see—and hear.

Last Wednesday night I spent the evening at K Bar—most enjoyable. C.K. was sick with a cold, hadn't been to work, but he seemed better. I walked with the children quite a long way exploring the rocks, then we sat on a hilltop behind the house and watched the full moon rise over the Dead Horse Mtns. Later, on the way to the Basin for Cokes we stopped long enough for C.K. to shoot a rattlesnake. Dr. Maxwell was at concessions, and I enjoyed eavesdropping on his conversation with C.K. Dr. Maxwell is an interesting talker and he told some treasure tales about this country I've never heard before. I'll have to tell you about the meteorite—the one that fell in 1918, at four o'clock in the afternoon. Dr. Maxwell talked to people from the Study Butte-Terlingua Creek area who saw it, and they agreed it fell east of the Chisos. He talked to a man from Boquillas and another who was at Hot Springs, and they said it fell between Glen Springs and Casa Grande. That fixed the meteorite about in Juniper Canyon, and Dr. Maxwell spent a week in the canyon searching for it but found no trace. Ray Miller, the only man who ever located it, is dead. He collected a sample for the American Museum of Natural History and reported that the piece he left in Big Bend weighed about twenty tons. What a find that would be! Goodnight, Art. Aileen

SEPTEMBER 29, 1953

Dear Mama,

Boots enjoyed the pickled peaches you sent back with me very much. Since he has the three boys I gave him two jars and gave Mae one. She liked them too. Boots is saving one jar until I go over for dinner, then we'll eat it.

Art sends you all his best regards. He seems to have approved of all of you as he mentions you in every letter. He likes his new rangering job. He is living in Buena Vista, Virginia, and has the Blue Ridge Parkway from that town to Shenandoah National Park. He writes that the people there have been extremely nice to him.

Last Friday night I went to an old-fashioned dance at the Dotts' place. It was the first dance I've been to since I met Art last April. I was afraid I'd forgotten how but not much. I've never danced so much nor with such a variety of humans. I spent the night with Mae and Steve (I mean what was left of the night) over in the Basin. We went into town next day and shopped. At about 10:30 P.M. on our way home we stopped at the Marathon hotel for a cup of coffee. The coffee shop was closed, but the hotel owners and some of the guests were having coffee, cake, and delicious candy in the kitchen, and they invited us to join them. Two of the men are working on the power line into the park. They said the park might have REA power by October—then no more depending on this little generator down here that runs constantly. Another man there is with an oil drilling company working on a ranch near Marathon. They've drilled eight thousand feet, he said, and have now brought in a new rig and are going deeper with hopes of striking abundant oil. One of the hotel owners said that the trouble with Marathon is the ranchers are all too rich. Some of those present hoped there won't be an oil boom, but a boom would certainly be exciting.

The Gullihers chased a panther into the park that had killed a sheep on their ranch. George had told them when that happened they could come in the park and kill it. So all today they were hunting the poor thing. Boots said this morning if they caught it we'd go over to the ranch this afternoon to see it. But no one has come to get me so the hunt must have been unsuccessful.

Gertrude, the other teacher, has been away for two weeks now. Some days I've taught all the children; other days we've had substitutes. We now know she won't be back until next week because she has had a throat operation. Mrs. Bledsoe, who lives here in Panther Junction, is teaching in her place now.

P.S. Sept. 30th - Had Scout meeting today. To Boots' and Nealie's for enchilada supper. Bob M., Slew, Uncle Roy, and Cecil were also there. Played dominoes all evening. Bob brought me home at eleven-thirty.

P.P.S. October 2 - Steve and Mae came here for supper tonight. Just after they left, all the Dotts and Bob M. came to invite me to go to Boquillas tomorrow in the daytime and to Marathon to a dance at night. I served them coffee, cookies, and the rest of Steve's pie.

P.P.P.S. October 4, Sunday - We did go to Boquillas in the rain yesterday. Got home from the Marathon dance at three this morning! AK

OCTOBER 6, 1953

Dear Art,

I planned to write you earlier tonight when my wits would be fresher, but Steve and Mae came for supper—I was glad to have them to eat with me—and before we finished, the board of trustees came for an unexpected meeting. Now it's ten, and I'm weary but I do want to get a letter off in tomorrow's mail.

We've had no rain during this latter part of the rainy season—even the creosote bushes are dead in the ranch pastures. George and Etta have produced a guide to "The Back Country." as they call it, which will provide help to the tenderfoots (feet?) who come to wander among the rattlesnakes, cacti, boulders, javelinas, etc.

Soon we'll have a new ranger and a new chief clerk, neither with school-age children, rumor says. Gertrude and I are glad. We're happy with things as they are—nineteen children.

The Dotts and I took the school supplies to Boquillas village last Saturday morning. We didn't linger because it was raining and we were afraid the river would rise while we were across. Boquillas has a new customs official now. We had heard he's very strict, so we went first to the "federal building" to explain our business and show our supplies. He was polite and helpful. He sent us to the ore camp to find the maestro, and I was glad because we had a chance to see the village and the camp beyond. How pitiful it was, especially in the drizzling rain—goats and burros hovering about the adobe houses, wet chickens walking in and out the doors, thin little children peeking out at us. The maestro came back to the school, and we unloaded everything (a box of clothes Nealie brought, too). His school, even with its dirt floor, was as clean as could be. He was delighted with everything. "Gracias, gracias" was all I could understand, but I knew what that meant.

The river didn't rise; the rain must have been a local shower, so we crossed safely and went by Hot Springs for refreshments and a chat with Etta.

Now, let's see, I haven't done anything else, I think. I did go out to dinner two nights last week. One was a "bachelor" dinner that happens every so often with most of the guests not really bachelors—Slew, Cecil, and Uncle Roy definitely not. Bob Mancil and I were the only real "bachelors" there, and he is debating marrying some California woman next month, and my heart is in Virginia, so it was a quiet evening.

Reece had all of Panther Junction to a dinner for Lon Garrison's birthday. We ate in the yard—barbecued goat (*cabrito*) and everything else delicious. Pete and Etta came up from Hot Springs too. We sang "Happy Birthday" to the guest of honor, and, naive soul that I am, when I saw him take off his glasses, I thought he was so moved by our singing he had to wipe his tears. Instead he kissed all the women and gave the men a Mexican greeting—kind of like two half hugs, given sideways, if that sounds possible.

It was so nice sitting in Shollys' yard by the fire and listening to the cottonwoods. Do you remember how they rustle and rustle in the slightest breeze? I thought about the time you and I stayed with Danny and Debbie, and we were eating on that little terrace in the dark. Danny was boasting about his bravery and how frightened Miss Kilgore would be if a panther came—and just then something with gleaming eyes passed by outside the gate. What a change of expression! I thought he would leap over the table into your lap. "What was that? What was that?" It wasn't Miss Kilgore who was so frightened! Do you remember?

Yesterday late I went out for a short walk. It was cold. I had to wear a coat and gloves but so wonderful for walking. As I went around the little hill just across the arroyo I came upon four deer. We were within a few feet of each other. I stopped still, and so did they until two of them bolted for the top of the hill. The two that stayed—a very light doe and a dark buck—kept inching closer to me and looking, looking, trying to figure out what I was. We watched each other about twenty minutes or so, when both of them raised their white tails and bounded to join the others. Aileen

OCTOBER 18, 1953

Dear Art,

Thanks for the scenic pamphlets you sent. Steve was here the afternoon they came. After reading them he is ready to visit you. (He and I had tea and cookies that day with Grandma Larsen, and then he helped me clean the school because he was stranded here in Panther Junction—couldn't find a ride home to the Basin).

I put the pamphlets out on the table in the school. I kept only one back for later, the one with the sketches of Jefferson's inventions. I thought it would mean more to the children when we study about him in history as our book talks at length about what an unusual man he was. I enjoyed reading them all, too.

We're at the end of our first six weeks. It's been very pleasant. I resolved coming back on the train that this would be the best year I've taught, as far as in my power. I'm happy that it seems to be working out that way.

I don't think I've told you that I'm now janitor of the San Vicente Common School #2 in District #1. The pres. of the board could get no one, so I decided if I could pay my rent that way, I'd be foolish not to. The board agreed to raise the janitor salary to $30 a month, and I agreed to take the job. This year I make $2700 teaching, which is far more than I'd have made in Alabama, even with three years experience.

You would love the smell of my apartment these days—licorice! Nealie and I bought a boxful of favors and candy for the children's Halloween party, and I have them stored here. Everything that's black and edible is licorice.

You and your camel out by the Windmill Road helped me teach my children something the other day. We were talking about nomadic herdsmen and how some of them have Bactrian camels and some have dromedary camels. I braced myself because I knew what was coming: What's the difference between them? I thought about you saying some day you were going out and push that camel over, and that he was a Bactrian varmint, and since I knew he has two humps, I answered the children with great authority, as if I knew all about such matters. Your Bactrian camel is still there—some day I'm going out and push him over.

I thought the enclosed picture might give you a laugh. It's all the pictures in one that we made the day Steve, Danny, and I went to Panther Springs. I don't know how it got in this shape. I distinctly remember rolling the film. The curse of the Apaches, no doubt, because we were trespassing in the Chisos. Maybe it's the mystery of the Phantom Mountains caught on film. When I look closely I think I see deer skeletons by the stagnant pools of Panther Springs; Comanches lurking behind the cactus; javelinas, panthers, meteorites, tenderfoot schoolteachers (by a tree where probably Pancho Villa was hanged), and poor boys whose fathers don't want them (Steve, I mean, not Danny). A rare print!

George came by the other afternoon to bring me a message from Inger Garrison, who was in Ft. Davis. He said he had a nice letter from you. I'm glad you wrote him. Aileen

OCTOBER 29, 1953

Dear Art,

Tomorrow night is our Halloween party. I've spent this night sorting prizes and planning games. The children are looking forward to a big time.

Even Steve has rigged up a costume. After the children's party the Casa Grande Club is having its October dance. Refreshments—cider and pumpkin pie.

We have enjoyed the colored leaves you sent. The children admired them very much. Do you know that Frank is the only one who has ever seen the trees turn, and he has seen only what East Texas has to offer, which isn't much. We mounted the leaves on green paper and posted them on the bulletin board. Thank you from all of us.

You have probably seen the Garrisons as they are in the east. If not, you will soon. They are in Washington, D.C., now. Lon came to school and made an interesting talk to the children about the ceremonies at the dam that day, and the lunch with the presidents. I am surprised that your papers carried it too, and I see the children's *Current Events* paper has a front-page story on it. The muddy old Rio Grande really made a stir. Yes, if you had been here we would have closed the school and away we would have gone, all of the children with us. Another adventure.

When you last wrote you said you thought you were homesick for Texas. You would have been sure you were if you could have smelled this desert after a storm we had the other night. Wonderful. What an unusual storm it was too. It came roaring down out of the Basin, great thunder, mighty winds, powerful lightning (auguring down all around but mostly pointed at the schoolhouse). Then a very violent, quick rain, and it was over. In a few minutes, here it came back from the other direction, and we had the same thing again. Since then the weather has been cold.

The biggest news with me is—I've tamed me a fox—nearly almost. He eats food when I throw it to him from the patio, and when I talk to him he doesn't run away any more. One night I forgot to put food out, and later when I turned the porch light on there he lay by a water pan curled up like a dog, flicking his black-tipped tail up and down, his eyes fixed on the door. I was so pleased! He got his supper right away.

I went to Hot Springs with the Shollys the other night. George was looking things over after another storm we had.

The panther you say you have there on the Blue Ridge Parkway is Alsate's spirit, I know. You can't escape him.

Aileen

NOVEMBER 10, 1953

Dear Mama,

We are getting REA power now, at long last, and the poles are ruining the beauty of Big Bend. Every time I look at the del Carmens, there stands a row of light poles. Green Gulch, one of the finest views on the road to the Basin, is defaced by a string of poles that cross the Chisos through a scenic gap.

I had a lovely weekend at Hot Springs with the Kochs—no electricity—we used kerosene lamps. It's so peaceful with only the sound of the river rushing over the rocks. Danny Sholly, Patty Koch and I wandered up and down the river all day Saturday, and Sunday I did mostly nothing. I drank several cups of Hot Springs water—it is very palatable. Did I tell you all that Lon Garrison had the water analyzed and it contains a chemical that is used in treating stomach ulcers?

During the course of the weekend all kinds of Big Bend characters showed up. A river rider, re-stationed at Lower Hot Springs since the re-outbreak of hoof-and-mouth disease in Mexico, came riding up out of the mesquite and cactus that borders the river when we were out front at Pete's store Sunday—handsome horse, western hat, leather chaps, boots, pearl-handled gun at his belt. He passed the time of day with us and then went on to Lower Hot Springs. Around suppertime George and Reece came from Panther Junction, then the Palmers from Boquillas Ranger Station. We had a pleasant time with good food and interesting talk.

Tweetie, the pretty parakeet I'm keeping for the Lundbergs, had a nightmare one midnight. She awakened me screaming and flinging herself about in her cage. Frightened me to death. A mouse must have been trying to get to her food. Aileen

NOVEMBER 15, 1953 - SUNDAY

Dear Everyone,

I never know what a day will bring forth here, and I'm only too willing to be lured away from my work. On Friday afternoon Nealie and Jack came for me to come eat a bean supper with them at Government Springs. Later we all went up to the Basin to join everyone who lives up there for an event they call a chivaree—what's done to newly married couples to torture them. Late at night we surrounded Bertyl and Jack Lewis' house with every kind of noise-maker possible, awakening them with a terrible din. We made them come outside, tousled and sleepy, in the chill night and ride burros! Then everybody danced past two!

Yesterday I spent the morning working at the school. Grandma Larsen came across the arroyo to invite me for fresh baked pastries and coffee (delicious!). That night I went with Shollys to Hot Springs for a party at Pete and Etta's. Left Hot Springs with the Dotts to go to their place where we danced till three in the morning. People here can make a party or a dance out of nothing and nobody!

Mr. Bob Cartilege, who has the old store at Castolon on the river, sent me a pair of ivory satin slippers from about 1900. They are so pretty and fit just right. The shelves of his store are stocked with old-fashioned clothes, hats, shoes, tools, implements, things from the days long before Castolon became a part of the park. It's like a museum. Boots and Nealie take me there often to visit Mr. Bob.

One night when the Dotts came over for pie and coffee we previewed a color film I'm planning to show in school. It is about how the things of nature express our Creator and shows scenes from some of the western parks (not Big Bend though)—beautiful and reverent. AK

NOVEMBER 16, 1953

Dear Art,

You must have been gone when the Garrisons came your way because last Wednesday they were in Georgia, on their way to the Everglades, according to a letter Leon Evans received from them today. This is the fourth week since they left. Grandma Larsen and I have enjoyed each other's company. I worked Saturday morning washing and housecleaning. So did she, then in the afternoon she came to invite me for sweet rolls—she had baked two large pans and then a small pan coated with sugar icing for us. They were so good—rich and delicious smelling. I did all the eating, I think; she mostly talked about Alaska and gold mining and fishing and Mr. Larsen. I enjoyed both the eating and the talking.

I've been sick for several weeks now, feeling most dreadful. That's so unusual I was convinced I was dying. It was a combination of things, I think—mental, physical, and spiritual. I am much better now. Etta and Pete had me down to Hot Springs for a weekend. That did wonders for me. Danny, Patty, and I wandered up and down the River all day Saturday catching minnows in Tornillo Creek, collecting snail shells and fossils, and soaking up that lovely, lazy sunshine. We hiked the original Comanche Trail on the Mexican side—the trail is worn deeper than our ankles—to the ruins of the Spanish Mission at San Vicente. It's in the mission door that you are to stand at sunrise on Easter morning if you want to find the treasure of the Chisos—the first rays of the sun will strike the entrance to the cave where the gold and silver are hidden. (Personally, I think that story sounds like something Harold made up).

I wish you could know how nice it is on the river now—cool breezes and warm sunshine. During the weekend all types of Big Bend characters and tourists wandered in and out—very entertaining. At night we had only the kerosene lamps, and I like their soft light.

Have you met or heard of Art Stupka, head naturalist at the Smoky Mountain Nat'l Pk? Etta and Pete spent their honeymoon in the Smokies, and this Mr. Stupka influenced Pete to come to Big Bend. They are good friends. Pete has a film he made while they were in the Smokies. Etta says it's beautiful. I hope I can see it some time.

Maggie Smith is back at San Vicente. She says her first night back she made $40 on wax. While I was at Hot Springs a pickup load of Federales came by and bought a few things at Pete's store. I would be frightened of them.

The Lundbergs are leaving the park, I'm sorry to say. Their children are a joy to teach, and C.K. and Ruth are supportive parents. C.K. will work with the Atomic Energy Commission, I believe, near Alamogordo. He told a most interesting story about being in the Dead Horse Mountains once with Jack Ketzle. You remember how vast and lonely the Dead Horse are so you can know how startled they were to hear a putt-putt noise like the motor of a one-cylinder engine. They looked over into the deep canyon below them. Nothing there. They persisted in searching for the source of the sound. Finally located it coming from a hole about the size of a lead pencil, a natural hole, not a bored hole. He and Jack estimated the rate of four hundred putt-putts per minute. They knew that there was oil drilling going on about eight miles south in Mexico and decided maybe the sound was traveling through the rocks. However, he's had second thoughts since then. Now he thinks the putt-putts may have been water dripping.

Mae and Steve left a week ago to be away until the 21st. Mae will probably marry Ray while they're gone. I feel so sad for her. She recognizes that the marriage will probably be a failure—Ray is drinking more than ever—but she says she loves him and that she can't bear to think about living alone any longer. Besides drinking, though, he doesn't get along well with Steve. Also he is a conventional Episcopalian, and you know how passionately devoted Mae and Steve are to the Jehovah's Witnesses. How can she even consider it?

Here lately I've been doing a bit of personal reading—something I haven't done in a long time. Usually schoolbooks take up my reading time. I've read two novels that have been on my shelf since I came here, and I'm reading the new translation of the Bible. It isn't as beautifully expressed as the King James, but I enjoy its simplicity. AK

DECEMBER 1, 1953

Dear Art,

Last mail day the photographs and the folder you sent on the Great Smoky Mtn. Park came. (They were missent to Big Wells, Texas). My favorites are the mill, the waterfalls, and the rail fence—how clear and beautiful they are! The Big Bend pictures you made before leaving the Park were a surprise, like orphans among those from the Smokies and the Parkway. I especially liked the one you made of Lost Mine Peak from Pine Canyon. That's a different view of Lost Mine from any I've ever seen. We must get down into that canyon! Now that Steve is back from his trip we're planning our Pine Canyon adventure. Wanted to go next Sunday, but Mr. Ivey at Lajitas is giving his annual barbecue then and we can't miss that.

I've meant to tell you that I've bought a camera similar to Mae's and Steve's. I decided I should spend a bit of money on picture taking. When I leave, I'd like to take some of Big Bend with me. This place has meant a lot to me—the wonderful coloring of the mountains, the spaciousness of it, and most especially the solitude. A walk in these Chisos foothills behind the school can cure almost anything that ever ails me. So I bought the camera, and the first roll of twenty pictures I made were all of the Sierra del Carmens—so beautiful then (November 11th) that I sat for hours on a hill back yonder watching the light change on them.

(How wild the wind is blowing tonight!)

I hope soon to make a picture of my foxes but night comes so early now it's hard to find a chance to photograph them. At three o'clock one morning I heard a great noise on my patio. When I turned the light on there was a fox wrestling with a milk bottle. I had forgotten to put food out, so I guess he was tired of waiting. I threw him the last of my bread, saving only a heel for breakfast. I hoped he'd be satisfied, but after a while he began struggling with the bottle again. I could hear him going farther and farther away. Next morning Jack found the bottle down the hill toward Headquarters, unbroken.

Do you still think you would like to work toward being a park naturalist? I hope you do. A ranger job is interesting, but I think being a naturalist would be even more so. It would have the advantages of rangering plus people wouldn't shoot at you for coming after them for killing deer they weren't supposed to kill. If Big Bend ever has a naturalist, I'll bet my cute red hat that's sitting on the closet shelf that Pete will be it. Observing him the weekends I've been at Hot Springs this year, and listening to him, I believe that's what he'd most like, and he is certainly qualified.

I still haven't seen a panther though I look and look. Lige Bledsoe saw a monstrous one this Sunday near the Gulliher ranch turnoff.

Tonight I had supper at Government Springs—fried venison, baked sweet potatoes, and chocolate pie—delicious. Boots, Jack, and Jimmy brought me home just a few minutes ago. It's 10:30 now—P.M. that is.

I could go on and on and on but there is school tomorrow, and Girl Scouts, too—a long day. Aileen

DECEMBER 7, 1953

Dear Art,

What a day we had at school! The gas tank turned up empty so we had no heat. The building was so cold we folk-danced to get warm. Then when everybody was panting we practiced our Christmas play. We wore our coats until late afternoon when the gas truck arrived and our furnace began working again.

Only nine more school days until the holidays. The children are beside themselves with excitement already. Every day we sing some of the Christmas songs. It's strange that we never grow tired of them.

Rex Ivey's barbecue at Lajitas was yesterday—a lovely day, very little wind, much sun. The willows along the river were golden, and the ore mixed in the mountain soil had turned the mountains all colors. We had wonderfully much delicious food: peppers, frijoles, salads, barbecued beef and goat, Spanish rice, that son-of-a-gun stew they all giggle about, and much more. We stayed for supper too (I went with the Dotts). Mrs. Ivey estimated they fed 550 persons at both meals. The music was unusually good—cultured cowboy played by a band from Marfa. They played most of those we used to hear when you were here plus some sad Spanish songs that just suit this place. Petra was there with Willie, her boyfriend. They danced only with each other. I worry that she will quit school to marry him.

Along the Santa Elena road we saw dead burros the rangers had shot. I was surprised they left them lying near the road for tourists to see. At Lajitas we played with a shaggy, cute baby burro.

On Saturday night I stayed at Shollys' house with an assortment of children while most of Panther Junction went to a dance in Marathon. They didn't come home until 4:30 A.M. so they were a little quiet at the barbecue. I met your friend Polo at the barbecue. He and Jesusita's father almost had a fight. Epifanio was there too. We left at eight. This afternoon Mickey told me we left too soon, things really got going about nine. I can imagine. It was wild enough when Nealie and I dragged Boots away.

I must go now. *Bueno Suerte*, Art. Good luck. That's the first Spanish I remember learning when I came to Big Bend—it was on a Lajitas road sign when I went to the Iveys' barbecue a year ago this December. Good night. Aileen

DECEMBER 13, 1953

Dear Art,

We've had an exciting weekend—it snowed in Big Bend Friday night. Everything has been beautiful in a different way. The ground wasn't completely covered, but we're all hoping for more and more this winter. The snow made no sound as it fell, though it seemed to. I was caught without film, but Steve made pictures in the Basin.

Ray was in the park this weekend. They came for me yesterday afternoon, and Steve showed his slides and mine and some Frank had. Steve has many good quality shots, I only a few, but I'm learning gradually. It was rather like making a debut to see my very own slides on the screen.

Thank you for the directions to Pine Canyon. Steve and I decided last night to postpone our trip until after Christmas. Frank expects to have a camera by then and may go with us. Yesterday as Steve and I sped up Green Gulch I was complaining about the string of power poles that ruin the scenery of the Gulch now. Suddenly the car began bucking all over the road. My first thought was, "Alsate's spirit likes the power poles!" When Steve managed to stop, we discovered we had a flat tire. While we struggled to fix it, Alsate, serenely sprinkled with snow, lay in full view.

I'm always thrilled to see the antelope that race across the flat just before Green Gulch—they are so swift and beautiful.   AK

JANUARY 3, 1954 - MARATHON, TEXAS

Dear Mama and Daddy and All,

I arrived here at 1:30 P.M. and stayed at the station until 8 P.M. waiting for someone to pick me up. No one came, and the few I knew of who might be going down to the park had already gone by the time I telephoned. I dragged my weary bones across the arroyo in the dark to find a room for the night.

Near the hotel I met Mr. Bob Cartilage (the one from Castolon who sent me the satin shoes). He had eaten, but he entertained me during my supper with his tales of the old days in the Big Bend.

Finally into my room, where I put up my hair, showered, and was ready to turn out the light after resigning myself to catching the mail bus down tomorrow and arriving at noon. (I was laughing to think of Gertrude when she got to school in the morning and found I hadn't returned). The phone interrupted my feeble laughter—long distance. Mae was calling from Ft. Stockton to tell me they were on their way down to Marathon and would see me at midnight. It's that time now, and I'm in the hotel lobby waiting.

Weatherwise this was a perfect Big Bend winter day—blue sky, brilliant sunshine, and just cool enough. Aileen

JANUARY 4, 1953 - BIG BEND - 11:05 P.M.

Dear Art,

What an adventure it was getting back to Big Bend. The train was on time, but nobody met me. I waited and waited because I was so sure someone would be around. When I realized I had to find my own way down to the park and began telephoning, Roy Lassiter and Slue had already gone down. The station agent tried to help me find someone, but he had no luck either. I went to the hotel resigned to catching the mail bus down at nine the next morning. I was too tired to laugh, but I couldn't help chuckling to think of Gertrude's reaction when she got to school and found I hadn't come back. Before I left Panther Junction for the holidays, she kept telling me to be sure to come back, that she wouldn't know what to do if I left her with all of the children. I think she was really worried even though I told her that I would abide by my contract no matter what jobs were offered me or what else might come up.

After eating supper I showered and had just stretched my weary bones on the bed when the phone rang. It was Mae. She and Ray had been delayed on their way down from Odessa but would pick me up about midnight. So I dressed again, and packed again, and went to the lobby to wait for them. I wrote Mama and Daddy while I waited so they would know I was all right.

About 12:30 Mae and Ray came, and we started on the endless road to Panther Junction. Everything seems to be going well with them. Mae is looking for a job in Odessa and has a good prospect now.

We arrived in the park by three and I was in bed by 3:30. Morning came too soon—I was awakened by a pounding on the door, and I could hear the children in the school. I was shocked to see the clock said ten minutes to eight! No time for breakfast. We had a busy, good day. The children were eager to get to work again. They told some of the things they had done during the holidays, and I showed them that wonderful assortment of things you sent them from the seashore. As I was taking the shells out piece by piece, I found the horehound stick candy you sent them. They had never heard of it before and thought it odd but enjoyed it very much.

Millard Ray brought me a beautiful panther paw this morning. I wish I could preserve it. The panther was killed at the Gulliher ranch, and Millard had them cut off the paw for me as I've always wished to see a lion. Sigh—this may be the nearest I'll ever get to a real live one.

Steve came over at lunch for a while, then he and Ray brought the parakeets back to me this afternoon. I tried to give them to Steve, but he refused because they aren't tame enough. I might be glad he didn't accept them during these long months ahead.

As soon as the school day was over and I had read the mail, I put out food and water for the animals. I never did see anything come, but the food is gone now so my foxes may still be here. Then I washed clothes—that took a long time. Then I put away the groceries Willie had brought and cleaned the refrigerator and turned it on. All this is very dull and routine—except the panther paw—and I hope you haven't fallen asleep.

I've noticed a sign along one of these Texas highways that says: "The faster you go the sooner you may be gone." That's just as true on those eastern highways you are traveling, so please remember!   Aileen

Millard Ray Dott holding the panther foot he brought to Miss Kilgore.

JANUARY 5, 1954 - BIG BEND - 10:00 P.M.

Dear Art,

Just a note to let you know I am thinking of you and the lovely visit we had during the holidays. I had quite a bit of mail awaiting me including a card and note from Col. Raborg and Liz in Laredo saying they will return to Big Bend in the spring. I wish you could be here too!

This was a beautiful, beautiful day. I think January must be the ideal time to be in Big Bend for I remember last January was just as lovely as these two days have been—cool, crisp air, a deluge of sunshine and the bluest sky.

I had to burn my panther foot today. How I hated to give up that magnificent paw, but it was deteriorating. I wanted to put it in the freezing unit of the refrigerator but the children were horrified.

Everyone of the children has enjoyed the shells, driftwood, etc., that you sent them from the seashore. Jack Dott thinks the sea serpent is a moray eel. Every day Frank begs me for the large piece of driftwood, but I can't part with it.

Must get some schoolwork done. Good night. Aileen

JANUARY 10, 1954 - SUNDAY - 9 P.M.

Dear Art,

This has been an excellent week in school for all of us. Socially I turned down my first invitation to a dance since my return—from the Evanses on Wednesday night. I had things I needed to get done at school, but Grandma Larsen came visiting and she knitted and I sewed and we both talked—mostly about Norway and Alaska and her experiences there.

On Thursday I was sick, from not enough rest for so long, I know, because I've been up till twelve every night since getting back after that endless train ride. As soon as school was out I went to bed and felt fine next morning. We've turned out scads of work this week—more than any other week in school, I think.

During the last play period Friday I went for the mail, read your letter and one from home, packed my nightie in my small bag, and all the children and I squeezed into Gertrude's car and went to the Basin. I was supposed to lead the

Girl Scouts up Lost Mine Trail on Saturday to complete requirements for the "Foot Traveler" badge, but we postponed it till next Saturday so Petra and Little Mary can go. I had sent Steve word I couldn't go to Pine Canyon because of the Scout hike, so I doubted that he would be expecting me but he heard me extricating myself from Gertrude's car (no easy task, we were so packed) and came bounding out of his house to meet me.

Patty and Frank joined us for a hike to the foot of the falls on Baldy (Vernon Bailey). They showed me where the men were stranded that you helped rescue. On our way to the falls we were walking in single file—Steve first, Frank, me, Patty coming last. Frank suddenly jumped out of line pointing to the spot just passed over by Steve—a rattlesnake! We hadn't been watching because this is January and no respectable rattlesnake should be out this time of year, not even in Big Bend. Steve and I made a picture of it while Frank poked it with a stick to make it look lively. Then the boys killed it. Patty and I sat on a rock at the foot of the waterfall while the boys climbed around a while on Baldy.

Friday night Mae cut my bangs. We fooled around and didn't get in bed until midnight, which was most unwise with the Pine Canyon trip ahead. Next morning Steve and I cooked breakfast, and I promised I would write you what a fine man he is becoming if he would write you about the delicious biscuits I made. I surprised myself, but they were an accident. We had no milk so I used water, and yummy! We ate all but two and Mae had those for her lunch.

As Steve and I started walking up the hill from the Basin, Pete Koch picked us up so by 8:30 we were already starting up Lost Mine trail. We made pictures all along the way—the views were so beautiful and the weather so perfect. After our noon lunch Steve took a siesta lying on a rock. I reclined in a crooked, double oak tree that had caught a collection of pine needles and oak leaves to make a perfect cushion.

On the canyon floor we found a large madrone lying crossways with "A. Green" carved on it and a date that looked to both of us like "1911." We were sure we had found a relic of Willie's ancestors, but when he brought the groceries this morning he said his family didn't come to this country till 1912. He thought the date must be 1917. However, when I came over from the Basin with the Kochs this morning, Pete said the date was 1911—he saw it when he was exploring the canyon. Did you see it when you were down there?

We reached the Pine Canyon falls about 1:30. The only water was in a few still pools. What a view from the falls! What a sheer drop! Up to this moment I had enjoyed the trip very much, but from then on it became a nightmare. As we stood at the top of the falls facing the Dead Horse Mtns, we went to the right looking for a way around the falls. We intended to reach the Hot Springs road and end up at my house. We descended into a side canyon which we thought would lead us out, clambering over rough, steep terrain where Steve went down first, then I lowered the canteen and cameras one by one on a string, then threw my shoes down and descended in my sock feet so I could get a toe-hold on the rocks.

We went down, down that perilous, narrow canyon until we came to a point so steep and sheer we knew we could go no farther. I looked up at those rock walls rising hundreds of feet above us and closing in. Then I looked down, down hundreds of feet to the bottom, and then out through an opening where way beyond I could see the wonderful open desert. I felt trapped—every crack in the walls overhead seemed ready to loose a huge rock on us. I was so tired, so tired, and as we sat there trying to think what to do, a cloud came overhead. We could see only a narrow strip of dark cloud, and rain began falling. We both thought about water roaring down the canyon—it was so narrow where we were there wasn't even a ledge we could climb on to escape the torrent. Then the wind began to blow. As it shook the trees it sounded like water rushing upon us. Then came the thunder, and you know how thunder echoes in a canyon. I was nearer to panic than I have ever been in my life, and I was trembling all over. Oh, Art, I was so scared.

Steve was frightened too, but he helped me by staying calm. I knew I couldn't go to pieces or all might be lost, so after we rested a while, we decided we would have to go back up that terrible way we had come down. Despite the roughness, the sharpness, and the thorns, I came out of that side canyon in my sock feet entirely because the rocks were now slippery with rain. I made myself give attention only to the spot I was working on at the moment, not look up or down, or think of anything else.

When we finally reached the top of the side canyon the rain had stopped and the strip of sky was blue again. We were still in deep shade, but when we got ourselves back in Pine Canyon, far up on the peaks we could see the sunlight. Steve kept saying, "I wish we would reach the sunlight," and I thought of that hymn you sometimes played on your harmonica about "heavenly sunlight, heavenly sunlight, flooding my soul with glory divine," and I knew what the words meant as never before. We had to rest often on the way back and took our time down Lost Mine trail. Everett, the clerk at headquarters, picked us up soon after we reached the road to the Basin, and we were at Mae's by 5 P.M. We had told her we'd be back by six if we didn't get out the other end of the canyon so we were glad not to have worried her.

We were in bed by eight that night. Every time I closed my eyes I found myself clinging to a sheer wall with all depth below me and all height above me and huge boulders ready to roll down on me. How terrible it was!

Today I am almost all right again, but I'll never climb any of Big Bend's mountains again or go in a chasm of any kind. I may sound childish, but I am trembling now to think of that trip. Not that I regret going into Pine Canyon, but I do regret going into that side canyon.

Grandma Larsen and Karen are alone at the Garrison house. Inger and Lon are in California with Karen's brother Lars who is on furlough. Tonight Grandma and Karen came over to visit me bringing delicious rice cream—rice, sugar, and vanilla mixed with whipped cream and slivered almonds—and some of Grandma Larsen's wonderful pastry. After they left I packed a box of Big Bend rocks to send to Buster, whom I taught in Alabama before coming here. I saw his mother during the holidays, and she said he is still enthusiastic about rocks ever since I taught a rock-and-mineral unit. I also packed a package of gifts from my students here for the Korean orphan I support. Then I worked some eighth-grade arithmetic, and now I'm writing letters.

I hope you don't worry as I am really all right now. Steve and I agreed not to tell anyone, not even his mother, about the side canyon horror, but I told him I was going to write you about it. Good night. Aileen

JANUARY 14, 1954

Dear Art,

We've had several days in a row that were so gray and foggy only the tops of Panther, Wright, and Pummel peaks showed. When I took my walk the rain was falling slowly, the air was cold, but the desert had that fragrance I know I'll never forget. When I came inside and put the light on, my little house was so warm and cozy, the dripping rain so drowsy and soothing.

Tuesday night Mae ate supper with me, and we went to the canasta party at Mrs. Bledsoe's. Mae was to be presented her wedding gift (an electric mixer) from the park people. No one had given Mae the least hint about the gift. Everyone wanted it to be a surprise—except Gertrude visited Mae beforehand and told all. Mae said she couldn't be a hypocrite and pretend not to know about it. She did very well though. Gertrude should be ashamed, tut, tut. But I guess it's impossible for her to hold her tongue.

When I first came back Gertrude tried to maneuver me into a private situation so she could question me about the holidays, but each time I managed to escape her. When she would come in my apartment I'd leave the door open so the children could hear what was said, and on the playground I kept close company with the children. But one morning she determined to quiz me— she left her children and stood with me and mine while we ate mid-morning lunch. Then as soon as my children drifted off to play she asked me if I saw you while I was gone. I said yes but nothing more. I consider those holidays our personal property, and I don't care to have them cheapened by gossip. To her other questions I made joking answers. Finally she laughed and said, "I know you don't want to tell me but I'm asking you anyway." Since that day she hasn't asked questions about you and me but about my family—do they own their home, what kind of house do they have, how old is the house, etc. Can you imagine such insatiable curiosity?

This afternoon Mrs. Larsen sent me word to come over the arroyo and see her double hibiscus blooming. I went, and Mrs. Bledsoe came too, and we had Mrs. Larsen's delicious cinnamon rolls with tea. Such a cook she is! She showed us some lovely silver her sister in Norway sent her. I've never seen a pattern as graceful.

Mrs. Bledsoe told me some interesting things about Study Butte and Terlingua. She taught in the Study Butte school for fourteen years.

While we females attended Girl Scout meeting at Irene Evans' house yesterday (we couldn't have our cook-out at Dugout because of the weather) Eligio, Jack, and Frank swept and dusted our schoolroom, emptied the waste baskets, disinfected and mopped the boys' bathroom for me. They had already gone when I came home and discovered what they had done. I was pleased that they would be so thoughtful.

The rain is really sho' 'nuff pouring down now. I wish you were here. We could sit with dignity on the sofa and discuss the flora and fauna of Big Bend. Good night. Aileen

JANUARY 16, 1954 - SATURDAY - 10:30 P.M.

Dear Art,

This has been one of the most beautiful days I ever saw in Big Bend—the bluest sky, the most golden sun, no wind, and a touch of chill in the air. I washed clothes this morning and was hanging them out when Boots and Jack came for me to go with them over the river road. I was eager to go, as I've never been on it, so I got my camera and away we went by Government Springs to pick up Nealie and the others.

Shall I tell you what I made pictures of? (those I can remember):

The man figure leaning against the sphinx at the Oak Creek Canyon Road; Santa Elena from the Castolon turn-off; Castolon Peak from Mr. Bob's store; the Mule Ears; the windmills and the old cotton patch with Santa Elena and Mesa de Anguila in the background; Mr. Bob and our group on his store porch.

The Evanses and Giles were at Castolon when we arrived. I was looking at the antique merchandise and that table of petrified wood and rocks when Mr. Bob took Nealie and Gloria Giles in the back room to fit them in a pair of those old-time shoes. (Remember the ivory satin pumps he sent me? Irene had chosen a similar pair for herself). That gave all of us a chance to see the rest of his store and boxes and boxes of interesting shoes.

After we were on our way again Boots showed us an outstanding Indian *metate* by the side of the road. He called it an *olla* (oy-ya). We built a fire by the river and cooked lunch. I made several pictures there.

We didn't linger after lunch, though we felt like taking a siesta, but headed for Viviana and the quicksilver mine. I made a picture of Cow Heaven, which I had seen on the map and wondered about, and a picture of the village of Viviana (deserted now), and the del Carmens from Viviana.

I forgot to tell you we stopped at the Johnson ranch and talked with them a while. I made a picture of the river there and picked up two pieces of calcite. A hill covered with agates was beside our lunching place. Boots found two for me that he judged to be good ones.

At San Vicente I made a picture of the Schotte Tower on the del Carmens from Mrs. Smith's road. A well-educated Japanese, Maggie says, is living at San Vicente now with his American foster mother. He is farming many acres of land on the river, planning to grow tomatoes, onions, and carrots. He's already set out some of them.

Maggie intends to open another hot springs for health bathing, this one across the river in Mexico. She wants to escape the U.S. health requirements. She is going to see the spring tomorrow and if she likes it she'll build a bath-house and develop the project for tourists. While we were there some Mexicans brought in $90 worth of wax. Do you remember the time we looked at her porch full of wax?

Next we crossed the river to Boquillas village to see if Boots could buy some beef. At the spring just over the river we found two Mexican children with their mother dipping water and pouring it into two large bags tied on each side of a burro. Each bag had a cow horn on a lower corner. Boots said that was to use when drawing water out of the bags. The bags looked like canvas, but Boots thought they were woven from lecheguilla. A fine dog was with them, and the mother grouped children, dog, and burro so I could make a picture.

The village, as usual, was depressing. The saloon appeared to be closed, but a bunch of men were collected to one side of it drinking and singing sad songs to the music of a guitar. Boots parked across the street from the saloon and left us sitting in the car while he went to talk to a man. Shortly, Petra's grandfather, Mecadio, came from across the road with bottles of beer (Carta Blanca!) for Nealie and me. We explained politely to him that we don't drink, thank you. He apologized over and over. When Boots came back, he said Nealie and I should have taken the beer and sipped from it to save Mecadio's feelings. He said Mecadio wanted to do something nice for us and suggested bringing us the beer. Boots didn't object. Nealie and I insisted that Boots should have explained to Mercadio that we didn't drink—Boots himself was the one who should have spared the old man's feelings. Boots drank one bottle of Mercadio's beer and Jack the other.

Away we went toward home after Boots arranged a rendezvous for tomorrow night at Maggie's with a man who is bringing him a whole calf. The river is full of river riders patrolling now, and I wonder how Boots thinks he can get away with this.

They brought me back to Panther Junction about seven. I brought in my clothes, put them away; ate supper, and am now writing letters. Aileen

January 16, 1954 - Saturday

Dear Daddy,

I was late getting home tonight, and I saw one of my foxes lurking in the greasewood waiting for food. As soon as I could, I set out his supper. However, he wasn't pleased with the food—crackers. He ate only two. I could see where his tongue wet the floor when he licked them up. I had two pieces of light bread, but I was saving them for my breakfast in the morning. The only other thing I had was some hard candy. I threw some of it on the patio (he was sitting patiently by the water pans). He came on the patio and chomped some of the candy. He couldn't handle it very well but stood waiting for something else. So I finally threw him my breakfast bread, and now I guess I'll have hot cakes.

Today I gave Tweetie and Sweetie to a new home in the Basin. The birds were not happy with me—I couldn't take up the time with them that they needed.

I washed this morning and was hanging out clothes when Boots came for me to go on the river with them. We went down the Santa Elena road until we came in sight of the canyon, then turned left and followed the river road from Castolon, Viviana, San Vicente, and Boquillas. We had a beautiful day for the trip. Down on the Johnson ranch about two o'clock we stopped and cooked lunch. We ended up in Mexico, in the little village of Boquillas, where the school is that we send supplies to.

January 18 - Monday - 10:05 P.M. Another lovely day. I cleaned the school, worked on some papers, and made lesson plans. This is exam week. Cooked supper and made cookies. Between jobs I watched the eclipse of the moon with my foxes.

I went to bed early last night for a change, about nine. I turned off the lamp and went over to open a porch window. Sitting in the moonlight on the corner of the patio was my favorite fox that always comes about eight. The other one comes earlier and usually eats most of the food. When I put the porch light on, it blinked its eyes but didn't get up until I threw out bread. Tonight I saved it a choice bone but so far it hasn't come, though the wilder one has come and eaten. AK

JANUARY 21, 1954 - BIG BEND - 7:15 P.M.

Dear Art,

We took most of our exams today. Only a few left for tomorrow. I suffered more than the children. They looked so comical, concentrating on their papers, in all sorts of positions and with all sorts of expressions, that I got the camera and made their picture.

We had two films yesterday afternoon, *Day is New*, which was about life in a large city in Mexico, and a beautiful color film on Yosemite Park. How the children marveled at all that water rushing among the rocks and down those lovely waterfalls—I did too for that matter. It seemed such a waste of precious water to us who have to count every drop.

I've not been doing much other than schoolwork lately. Tuesday night Boots, Nealie, etc., and Mae and Steve came over to preview the two films with me and to have cookies and coffee. Steve has some new slides. Mine of Pine Canyon should be back in tomorrow's mail. We hope to show them at Government Springs tomorrow night when Mae is giving Nealie a permanent, and we're all invited for supper.

Probably we'll cancel our Girl Scout hike again Saturday because of weather. A norther is coming in—much dust—the del Carmens are invisible, the Dead Horse almost so. I'm to go to Hot Springs Sunday for the day with Patty, Etta, and Pete.

One thing I regret is that you and I never watched the moon rise over the Dead Horse Mountains from my patio. I think the Dead Horse are usually dull mountains, but the moon rising over them, just to the left of Horse Head, is a breathtaking sight I've seen only twice—soon after I came to Big Bend and the night after the eclipse this week. You see a great golden radiance, long before the moon itself, and then that first bit of moon, and gradually the full power of the whole moon. But you and I saw it rise over the del Carmens once when we were coming from Hot Springs with Jimmy and Millard Ray in the back seat, remember? That was funny! Aileen

JANUARY 26, 1954 - TUESDAY NIGHT - 7:45

Dear Art,

What a wonderful day this has been, weather and everything. The day was like spring in Big Bend—wasps and yellow jackets used our schoolroom for a thoroughfare—in the windows and out the open door or vice versa, and every time one of insects paused to look at a child, said child would shriek and thrash the air. Spring fever is coming too soon. I made out report cards this afternoon (they're due tomorrow) and almost everybody is getting his best card this time. I told them if they'd only work the next eighteen weeks the way they've worked the three weeks since Christmas, I'd be most happy. Some of them grinned and said they made a New Year's resolution to work harder in school. I'm most fond of each of them, bless their hearts.

The news clippings you send are very interesting. It's strange how they always fit into school sooner or later. Today in reading, the eighth grade had a story about Mark Twain. Because of your clippings I could tell them about his house in New York, scheduled to be torn down, and about the radio program on his life. Amazingly, Frank blossomed out and told us about the program and how much he enjoyed hearing it. He listens often to the radio and tells us interesting tidbits. His interests are broadening and he is sure enough growing up.

On Saturday I did schoolwork and housework and made cookies. On Sunday I went to Hot Springs and had a lovely, restful day with the Kochs. We made a mesquite wood fire in the big room (the fireplace sits cater-cornered in a corner, remember?) and sat by the fire in the early morning. After things warmed up we went out walking in the sun—down to where the river goes over the rocks and makes that murmuring sound.

While we were out there the river rider came by on that horse I love. He is a bay with a blaze face, and the river rider has papers on him—he's a real

Cooking lunch at Hot Springs with the Koch family.

quarter horse. Horses can tell, I think, when you like them. Patty and I scratched him and fed him leaves and talked to him, and he would smell my hair and nibble at my ear with those wonderful soft lips and rub against my face. How much I liked him! (The river rider was squatted under a bush smoking a cigarette all this while. If he hadn't kept such a close watch on us Patty and I would have ridden Chungo.) The river rider stayed for lunch, and while he socialized with Pete and Etta, Patty and I took a box and went around collecting dead mesquite leaves that Chungo liked immensely. We brought him water in a dishpan from the pump, and we sat and admired every move he made. I even liked the way he smelled.

We had steaks for lunch—Pete broils them just right—and we ate at the big table under the cottonwood tree. We saw the little Mexican boys drive their goats to the river to drink; then the boys drank from the muddy river too. The beautiful day affected the goats and the boys—they frolicked so nimbly and made all kinds of exuberant noises. How happy they were! (The cotton-woods are blooming and leafing out!)

After we cleaned up the lunch things I went with Patty to her stone house on the hilltop. She had tied up the hammock for me and placed cushions under

Miss Kilgore and Patty Koch at the Hot Springs tourist rooms. Miss Kilgore slept in the room to the right and reported that the wind rattled the river canes on the roof all night.

it in case of collapse, and I spent the rest of the afternoon in it looking at the blue, blue piece of sky and the tan rocky hill, and thinking of you—only you, not even of Chungo, though now I think to write you of him. I had been there for hours when Mae, Steve, and Jack came. At sunset Patty and I went home with them (I to Panther Junction, Patty to the Basin), stopping along the way to make a picture or two or three. Aileen

JANUARY 28, 1954

Dear Art,

It is three o'clock now. The children and Gertrude have gone—quiet. We've had a beautiful summer day, and that isn't good for schoolwork. Everybody dreams a bit, even the teacher, and it's hard to concentrate on book learning. We had two movies (in color) this afternoon. First was *Bobolink and Bluejay* (the eastern bluejay). Immediately the children noticed the jay in the film was different from the Big Bend jay, but to me it looked like an old friend. (I even like to hear them shrieking in the woods.) The second film was about a lake in Mexico, *Patzcuaro* (lake of delight), and was most beautiful—the fishermen with their butterfly nets going out in the lake, the cathedral, and plants, and people in the market.

Mae and Steve are coming over tonight for supper and to see the two movies. Steve will enjoy the Mexico one I know because of the photography. His life has been troubled lately. He is in disfavor with park officials for several reasons, and now they've asked Mae not to let him drive in the park. I've never seen him drive recklessly, but I've seen park adults who have driven so, and as I told Nealie the other day: I've never seen or heard Steve do or say anything out of the way. He is a good boy, but a woman in the Basin has told all the mothers of the park that he acts improperly with the smaller boys. She told similar stories last year, and now she is reviving them. I wish Mae would take Steve away to a different environment for his sake. Poor Steve. Aileen

JANUARY 31, 1954

Dear Mama and Daddy:

This has been a gray day in Big Bend, dense fog and a cold wind blowing out of the north. I've just returned from a long walk back toward the mountains—very enjoyable though I didn't see a single animal. Now (6:30 P.M.) I'm cooking my supper—delicious onion and potato soup.

The past week was a quiet one. Schoolwork still goes well though we've been back four weeks. I hope the children's morale stays this high. Some of the days were beautiful summer days, and I could see right away their minds were beginning to drift the way they do toward the end of school. Mine, too. But now we're getting winter weather back maybe we'll stay in the groove.

On Wednesday afternoon we had our Girl Scout cookout at Dugout. Hot dogs and hot chocolate. I didn't have to cook supper that night.

Yesterday I went with the Dotts to Crotan Springs. Boots and the boys fished while Nealie and I looked for Indian arrowheads. I collected many beautiful chippings, but Nealie found the largest and prettiest Big Bend arrowhead I've seen. In the big rocks there around the old adobe ranch house were lots of corn grinding holes left by the Indians.

I have many pretty slides from the trips I've made since coming back to the park. We showed our slides, Steve and I, at Nealie's one night on a borrowed projector.

February 7, 1954 - Sunday. Haven't mailed this letter yet. Willie did me a great favor today. On Friday night I defrosted my refrigerator and forgot to turn it back on. I left here Saturday morning without discovering that oversight, went with the Girl Scouts on a hike up Lost Mine trail, went from there to Mae's to spend the night, and when Willie came to bring my groceries he found a hot and defrosted box. He turned it on before putting in my week's supply of milk and vegetables and took ice out of his grocery van to pile in the refrigerator so there'd be no chance of anything spoiling. Fortunately I had had only a frozen fryer left from the previous week, and it hadn't spoiled.

This morning Steve, Frank, and I took a hike up on the side of Casa Grande, at the Basin, to Kibbee Springs. Some reputable men reported seeing two bears near there last week, and we hoped to make pictures of them or of a panther, but no luck.

When Mae brought me home this afternoon she had a flat. I changed her tire for her—reminded me of my mechanic days. After that I cleaned the school and dug around and watered the two Spanish daggers in my yard. They are almost ready to bloom.

Must go to bed now to get strength for another week. AK

FEBRUARY 7, 1954 - 10:10 P.M.

Dear Art,

Here is the end of another beautiful Big Bend weekend, with just enough wind and dust to remind us that soon the wind will really begin to blow and not let up till May.

Do you remember the two Spanish daggers by the watering pans? They are budding now. I've dug around them and watered them thoroughly, hoping to help them out a little. It seems early for them to bloom. I remember last year when they bloomed the deer came immediately and ate the blossoms. Not for a while this year, I hope.

All the plants may do better this spring because of the slight snow before I left and the heavier one during the holidays. There has been little rain though.

Yesterday I took the Scouts on the five-mile hike we're supposed to do for our Foot Traveler's badge. We went on the Lost Mine trail and beyond to make the required mileage. Ate lunch at the top while we watched all those fascinating caves that can be seen from there. We saw no animals though Patty, Petra, and I had our cameras.

I spent the night with Mae and had an enjoyable time as usual. She is trying to find Ray a job in the park but nothing seems available. Bo and Gertrude came over to visit after supper, and Bo analyzed our handwriting according to a magazine article he read. We had many laughs because some of the traits fit us so well. This morning, before I was out of bed, Steve was studying the letter you wrote him, analyzing your writing. He found only good things about you. Nothing bad as some of us had. Probably he will tell you when he writes.

Bo and Gertrude brought me an income tax form from town, but it was a long one, and I don't want to struggle with it. I'll have to dig up another one right away as time is getting so short I'm worried. I'd hate to go to jail if that's what they do to you for being late. Aileen

FEBRUARY 11, 1954 - THURSDAY NIGHT

Dear Art,

Tonight is like summer, and I'd rather be sitting on the patio watching the Spanish daggers and the animals than in here with the eighth grade's Revolutionary War and the sixth grade's War-Between-the-States, and the seventh grade's agriculture, but they must be tended to.

We had a film yesterday, *Trees for Tomorrow*, about the need for conserving our forests, replanting, selective cutting, and care with fire. We had two other films, both about Jan Paderewski. I was doubtful about the children's reaction to him as I remember they were bored with José Iturbi last year. These films showed Paderewski not long before his death playing Chopin's "Polonaise," his own minuet, and Beethoven's so-fragile "Moonlight Sonata." What a marvelous face he had, what a wonderful pianist—and the children were spellbound. We saw the films twice, and if I weren't afraid to sit in the dark out in the schoolhouse I'd see them again.

Tonight I've baked cookies. While I was working away there came a loud and very startling knock on my door going into the school. Mr. Evans and Mr. Giles had come for the projector. I didn't dream anybody was near. Did I ever tell you how much I appreciated you always calling my name as you approached my house? Not many people do, but it's very thoughtful.

Now I must tend to the wars. Aileen

FEBRUARY 13, 1954 - 8:10 P.M.

Dear Art,

I went to Government Springs with Gertrude and her commuters as soon as school was out. I had supper with the Dotts, and then we went to the ranch for a pleasant evening of sitting and talking. Fred G. told two stories about Santiago Peak that I hope not to forget before I see you—gold, silver, caves, Indians with cholera, and everything. We came home rather early, and before going to bed I read your letter again and the clippings. I enjoyed all of them, but especially the Havasupai Indian clipping. In the film we had about Grand Canyon we saw pictures, in color, of their beautiful valley and the way they live and some of their dances. I'll share that clipping with the children.

Why do you keep asking if I am well? Do you suspect I'm not? For the last two weeks I've not been, but I'm better now and hope to be well by Monday. I've a cold like I've never had before, a deep one with much coughing. I've been going to bed at a decent hour, spending a lot of time outdoors, and everything else that's supposed to be healthy but I'm just now getting better. Inger gave me some pills with morphine in them to make me sleep, Boots gave me rum with orders to take a hot toddy every night before I retire. I take vitamins and drink fruit juice, too, of my own accord.

The deer ate my Spanish dagger blossom the night I wrote you about it (Thurs).

Sunday afternoon: I am much better today. I told George I would like a panther rug before I leave in May. He said he would get one for me but it would cost $40 or more. I told him that was all right but I wanted its head, tail, and all four feet attached. George gave the rug that he's already had made to the rancher who killed the lion, but he said the taxidermist did a poor job on it. He knows a better place to send mine, he says.

A tourist saw a bear near Casa Grande, and Dr. Maxwell found a grown bear's track on Lost Mine trail. I don't understand why I never see any of them—it's the company I travel in, I think—too noisy. I'm going to start going alone exclusively. When we were walking to Kibbee Springs, Frank and Steve galloped in front talking, laughing, knocking rocks, and making all kinds of noises. I was trailing along behind like a mouse, not saying a word. Just before we reached the spring, one of them turned around and said, "Now if we can just get Miss Kilgore to keep her mouth shut we might see something." I was thunderstruck but didn't take time to defend myself for fear I might miss seeing a critter. I hoped more for a panther than a bear but there was nothing.
Aileen

P.S. Two of Fred's treasure tales: A sheepherder found a cave with four hundred Indians sitting among sixty kegs of silver. They had died of cholera. The sheepherder who found them died within a week. (I failed to ask what period of time this was in the past.) One of Fred's own sheepherders disappeared leaving his bedroll, et al, behind. Years later another sheepherder came and told Fred that before he disappeared, the missing herder had found a cave. The entrance was under a large rock with a cross on it. The first Mexican had emptied the flour out of his food sack onto the ground and filled it with silver. Leaving everything he owned at his camp, he went to the river and sailed down it to Del Rio. He's now in an asylum. The second Mexican spent years herding for Fred and looking for the cave. I may have some of this confused because one story involved gold stolen by the Indians from two Englishmen who had come to buy land but who died of cholera.

FEBRUARY 16, 1954 - TUESDAY - 8:10 P.M.

Dear Art,

Before starting this letter I looked out on the porch and there sat my favorite fox waiting patiently. From my cache of bread I took two pieces and held one out to him. He came over, took it from my hand, and dashed away.

That's the first time he has ever done that. Always before when I would hold food in my hand he'd want to come but just couldn't make up his mind. As the days are noticeably longer now maybe soon I can take his picture.

You asked about wet Mexicans. I know more about the situation from reading *The New York Times* than from what I hear locally. I have meant to tell you about Candilladio, the wetback who lives at the Gulliher ranch. Last year he lived in a tent behind the barn. Then he married a girl from Boquillas, who is over here illegally also. She was so afraid of being caught by the Border Patrol that they moved their tent up in a wild canyon behind the ranch. She is very young, can't speak English, and is going to have a baby in about two months. There is nobody to be a friend to her. Nita (at the ranch) who doesn't speak Spanish, laughed and told Nealie and me that she hoped she didn't end up acting as doctor for her. How tragic if their living conditions at the ranch are an improvement over what they would have had in Mexico.

Some of the park people went through Boquillas Canyon last weekend in rubber rafts. They counted twenty wax camps within the canyon, one of them on the U.S. side. George, Leon Evans, and Lon destroyed the one on our side, but they merely explored those on the Mexican side.

Frank is having his tonsils out this week. I have only five children, but we still don't have time enough for everything. Tomorrow I'm showing three films—*Portugal, Pan American Bazaar,* and *Igor Gorin,* a baritone, singing excerpts from operas. Aileen

FEBRUARY 19, 1954 - FRIDAY NIGHT - 10 O'CLOCK

Dear Art,

This has been a good week in Big Bend, weather, and events. School went smoothly except in the last few minutes this afternoon Erozmo and Millard Ray tore into each other. If I am completely well Tuesday, as I hope to be, I'll have them in organized games again, which always keeps them out of trouble.

I've just fed my favorite fox. He won't eat crackers as the other foxes do— but he loves cookies, loaf bread, and lumps of brown sugar. And Petra's agriculture book says foxes are carnivores! Last night when I went to bed he hadn't come for supper. At 4:15 this morning a milk bottle overturning on the porch awakened me. When I looked out he was sitting on the porch watching the door. He has learned that by making a noise he can get me to the door with food, as that is the third time he has overturned a bottle in the night.

At lunch yesterday two coyotes, looking like large police dogs, one gray, the other tan, trotted slowly through Panther Junction.

This afternoon Steve and Danny came up for a while before Steve and Mae left for Odessa. They are picking up Ray there and going on to New Mexico to investigate a school for Steve. He was in a sour frame of mind, but I expect he will be more enthusiastic when he sees the school.

At suppertime Jack and Millard Ray rode over from Government Springs on Jack's bicycle. They stayed long enough for milk and cake, but I sent them home before they had rested enough because dark was coming and they had no light on the bicycle. Aileen

FEBRUARY 26, 1954 - 7:20 P.M.

Dear Art,

I'm sorry I've neglected to tell you that I have a light meter, but to tell you the truth I'd forgotten about it until recently. I ordered it with the camera, but when it came it had no needle gauge. I sent it back, and the next one had no needle gauge either! I returned it, and the third one came the day I left for the holidays. In the confusion of packing and producing the play and accepting and giving Christmas presents, I only took time to check the wholeness of the meter and put it away. Just recently I got it out when I went on a long walk toward Pummel Peak. I parked myself back there on a hill in hopes of getting some deer pictures, and while waiting I studied out how to work the meter. Haven't used it yet, but next Tuesday afternoon when the Dotts and I go to the ranch I intend to use it. They will be shearing then, and I remember how colorful it was last year.

My special fox did the most cunning thing the other night. I turned on the patio light, and there he sat calmly blinking. I usually open the inside door to let him know I see him, and while I get his food he comes over and watches me through the screen door. When I put the food out he backs away to the middle of the patio. This night, though, I spoke to him through the window but forgot to open the door. When I turned from getting his food, there he was up on the porch chair looking in the window!

Last night I put out for him a piece of bread, a piece of cheese, and a handful of crackers. Out of that pile of food he selected the bread, held it in his mouth and picked up the cheese too, and went away. He just won't eat crackers though the others seem to like them. Sometimes that's all I have to give him, especially toward the end of the week. I do look for a lion, Art, and I carry my camera everywhere. I've given the lions every opportunity to show themselves to me, but no luck. I won't give up, not even my last day here.

Last Monday I wrote Glenn Burgess asking his advice about accessories for the camera. In *The New York Times* I saw where a new book is out on slide-picture taking, and I asked him about that as I'd like to read such a book. He is getting me duplicates of some of Steve's best slides, those he made in the late summer of century plants, columbines, etc., and those of the snow while I was away Christmas. Seven dollars worth, but you will like them as I do.

I've thirty-six exposures away being developed now. Since Lajitas, when Glenn suggested I cut down on the lens opening because of the tremendous amount of reflected light from the desert and rocks, my slides have been a richer color. Some of the Pine Canyon ones you will really like, I think. I try to make the pictures show my love for Big Bend. I believe some of them do show that a loving hand and eye made them.

I appreciate your criticism. I need it. Pete is always so busy when I'm down at Hot Springs that I don't like to bother him. He's taken over Harold's postcard route and on weekends he is packing and preparing for the two-day trip. Jean Palmer, from Boquillas, keeps the store when he's away. I'm sending a clipping from today's *Alpine Avalanche* about him.

You should see the plant I brought out of Pine Canyon—a fast-growing, waxy plant that is green, low and spreading, and is as pretty as a blossom. I've not seen another one like it anywhere. Willie said he thought he had seen it before. He believes it may have a red blossom. I set it out in a pot, and I hope to bring it home with me. In Pine Canyon it was growing with one big root from under a rock.

Willie is as kind as ever. I told you about the good deed he did when I was over in the Basin and left my refrigerator off, didn't I? Well, last Sunday he left me forty lemons. I was thunderstruck when I looked in the sack—I had ordered four! I decided to keep them all because I like lemons and as I had such a bad cold I needed to doctor myself with them. But do you know, by Tuesday he had heard about it in Marathon, though I had told only one soul, and he sent me word he would take them back this coming Sunday! I've a picture of Willie and his grocery rig, an absolutely essential part of the Big Bend scene. And he told me his gorgeous white cat has a handsome new family.

Petra tells me every day about a beautiful pear tree in full blossom over at the Grapevine Hills. It would be worth driving miles to see a pear tree in bloom. Spring is here. The cottonwood trees are greening. The air is mild tonight, though there is wind, and I have the door open.

My slide you mentioned of Ft. Davis is one I like too, but Steve thinks it is aimless. I wish I had thought of using something to show the size of the grinding stone. The sun was hazy that day too. I think I'll have a better one of the Croton Springs grinding stones. The sun was brighter, and in one of them Jimmy Dott is reaching down in the grinding hole. Even the round rock used for grinding was there.

Grandma Larsen is going away, I suppose in May as she said she was going about the time I'd be leaving. She said she didn't want anyone to know but asked me to take her to the Indian camp across the arroyo so she can collect some chippings and maybe an arrowhead for her other grandchildren.

She brought me some delicious bread one afternoon. You and I aren't the only ones who realize that the spirits of the Chisos carry tales—she does too, and so did Ruth and C.K. Ruth came over one morning and asked me to witness their signature on an insurance form. They had to borrow money in order to move to New Mexico, and she said they didn't want all of Big Bend to know about it. Aileen

MARCH 2, 1954 - TUESDAY - 11:30 P.M.

Dear Art,

I've fed the fox, my main one, put out water for the animals, fixed my grocery list, and gotten some film ready for the mail tomorrow, and I should be taking my bath—but I will write you a note.

I am so tired, so tired. We had Spanish class here last night (George is teaching it), and I arose at 6:30 this morning to put the school in order again. Last night was the first class meeting, and thirteen of us attended counting George. We are using the Border Patrol book.

My students are taking six-weeks exams. That is always a strain, more so on me, I think, than on the children because I'm so anxious for them to do well. Today is Texas Independence Day—1836. Before I leave I want to buy a Texas history like the one the seventh grade uses. It's very exciting, especially the first half. The children saved coupons from notebook paper, and I furnished the quarter to order a portfolio of Texas heroes. The pictures are handsomely done. We posted them on our walls.

We are having a norther with much dust. Lone Mtn was hardly visible from the school. Very cold. I wore the western boots Karen gave me to the ranch and your socks and was very comfortable. On the way over I think I got some good shots of black-tail deer in Paint Gap near Dripping Springs. One buck was close, but in the shade, and they blend into the rocks completely!

Everybody at the ranch was working hard. Most of the goats (angora) had been sheared, but there were hundreds of sheep left to do. I used all my film though the air was thick with dust and the sun was weak and low. If only there was enough light I should have some good pictures!

I was back here by 9:30 and dashed over to Garrisons' to the ceramics class Inger is teaching. I was sorry to be late but the ranch trip was especially for me to make pictures of the shearing, so I felt I couldn't miss the chance. Anyway, Inger had said to come on over when I got home and I did. They had made some interesting plaques and plaster of Paris bats to work their clay on in the future. I'll go over before next class and make mine so I won't be too far behind.

You remember we made pottery in Girl Scouts. Inger came over Sunday to ask me to come see how they looked after the glaze firing. I was eager to see, and when we were getting out of the car at her house she grinned and said, "I guess you know yours was the perfect one." I didn't, but I knew it had been a labor of love—I've wanted to do ceramics for years, and I was glad she thought my bowl turned out well. We set about re-glazing the others so they could be fired again before Scout meeting to keep the girls from being disappointed by the messy glazing jobs they did. Irene decided not to do hers again, and Karen's was quite nice, too.

Saturday night I had dinner at the Garrisons' and as always had an interesting evening. Dr. Wilson, a paleontologist who is working on fossils here now, was there, and the president of the El Paso Chamber of Commerce with his wife, and the Chamber of Commerce photographer, and in addition the Shollys and Evanses. Shollys, Evanses, and Garrisons showed the slides they made when they went through Boquillas Canyon. Some beautiful shots.

You are right when you say I am with good people. They have done so many thoughtful things for me. I am overwhelmed when I think about it. Especially have the Garrisons, the Shollys, the Dotts, and Mae and Steve. They really looked after me when I was sick—even Danny. One afternoon he walked George's horse up here (they had him at the house for a few days) for me to see, and one Sunday he came up and asked me to go walking with him. Most people are wonderful, aren't they—and life is wonderful, isn't it, Art?

Last night I showed my Pine Canyon plant to George hoping he could identify it. Before he saw it, I had jokingly told him that it was rare. When he looked at it his expression changed to one of great interest and he said, "It is rare." No one in Spanish class could identify it. Byram said he thought Willie was right in saying it had a red blossom. It is a succulent, says Inger; fleshy, says George, though I had described it to him as being "meaty." All agreed it was beautiful. The pointed leaves are so arranged that they make one large green-petaled flower. As soon as the sun shines brightly through this dust I want to make its picture so if something happens to keep me from taking it out of Big Bend I'll at least have a likeness. I have two pieces of sturdy cholla on the patio, saving to bring out with me in case I don't find handsomer pieces. They are from one of the hills in front of Panther and Wright Peaks. Aileen

MARCH 10, 1954 - 11:00 P.M.

Dear Art,

I saw a panther—I saw a panther!! Just now coming through Green Gulch! We had been talking about lions, and suddenly this one appeared on the left of the road, only a few feet from us. Reece turned the car crosswise of the road, and we examined it in the headlights. It faced us—we could clearly see the unmistakable rounded ears and that beautiful tawny color. After several seconds watching us it turned lengthwise and moved off into the brush without any particular hurry. From nose-tip to tail-tip it must have been about nine feet—not over that I think.

We were on our way home to Panther Junction from a barbecue in the Basin that started at 5:30. I went with Mae and Steve and planned to leave immediately afterward but had no transportation because Steve broke his wrist when he and the children were playing after supper. We were all so sorry because he was included in the Boquillas Canyon trip this coming weekend. When I saw him after he had been given first aid the first thing he said was: "I won't get to go." George took Mae and Steve into Alpine in a government car. Mae has had so much bad luck. She missed taking Steve to the school in New Mexico because she and Steve took sick in Odessa. She also lost a week from work and still isn't well.

I could sympathize with Steve because I'm also invited on the Boquillas Canyon trip, and I know how I'd feel if I had to miss it. I've been too excited to concentrate ever since Monday night after Spanish class when I found out I could go. This is Pat Miller's group going through—Pat, Mildred, Frank and his parents (Doris and Stanley), Gloria and Bob Giles, Gloria's mother, and the Castolon ranger, Bob Heying. (Sure enough the camera is going with me.)

You'll be as shocked as the rest of Big Bend at what happened to Bob and Lynn Heying. They seemed so perfectly matched in every way, and I thought Lynn was happy in Big Bend, living at Castolon and taking painting lessons from that tourist. But Bob came back from leave in January without her and said they were already divorced. We aren't recovered yet.

Gertrude and I had a surprise Monday—Bill, Jess, and Joyce enrolled again in our school. The Marathon school had promoted them to fifth grade so they are in Eligio's and Patty's class and are considerably behind in their studies.

Rattlesnakes are the only reason I'm reluctant for warm weather to come again. This morning we discovered one outside Gertrude's playground door, dead, but limber and still warm. The head was mashed. I can't puzzle out how it could have happened since all the children appeared to be innocent of any trick.

Last Friday two carloads of us went to Alpine to attend the ballet—a wonderful evening. We ate supper at the restaurant across from the college. I was at a table by the window where you and I once sat. After supper we went to Dr. and Mrs. Wildenthal's at the college for dessert. You would have liked it— cake and chocolaty ice cream mixed in an attractive and tasty way. The program interested all of us for various reasons: Etta noted ideas she can use for costumes in the program she's planning for the Basin ballet class in May. The children and Inger and I were spellbound by the music and the expressive movements. Afterwards in Marathon we stopped briefly at Rene's and Willie's for coffee before starting down the long road to Big Bend. The only life we saw along the way was a jackrabbit or two. Out of our car Frank stayed behind in Alpine and Danny in Marathon, so Karen stretched out in the back seat and slept. Inger, driving, and I talked mostly about the plans for the park dedication next October, and hers and Lon's life in the Park Service. She said, "Aileen, if you ever decide to become a Park Service wife, I'm sure you will enjoy it." I told her I was sure I would from what I had observed of their life in Big Bend.

Sunday afternoon the Dotts took me to the ranch. Gullihers had butchered a calf. We sat around in the pen and watched (I stayed away until they had the calf peeled). They gifted me with a big block of steak meat, and it is delicious.

To ceramics class tomorrow night at Inger's, and early to bed Friday night. The Boquillas Canyon crew meets at seven Saturday morning at the Giles' house in Panther Junction. Mae is lending me her sleeping bag. I'm planning to wear warm clothes. AK

MARCH 13, 1954 - PANTHER JUNCTION - 5:35 P.M.

Dear Art,

I wonder if you received a letter from me today. I wrote you about the panther I saw and sent it into town by Stanley on Thursday instead of waiting for our mail Friday. I couldn't wait to tell you!

This afternoon I am alone in my house, shut in from the rest of the world by the worst dust storm I've ever seen here. Panther, Wright, and Pummel peaks are invisible, so is Lone Mountain. But I'm not lonely for people. I've been with scads of people all day (since a quarter of seven this morning).

Our canyon trip had to be postponed, but what an adventure we had before the postponement! As planned, I was up before six this morning. One other light showed in Panther Junction—at the Giles' house. About ten of seven, after fixing my lunch for today and tomorrow and collecting my supplies and the camera, I hiked over there. During the night the weather had changed from sultry hot to very cold and windy. Some dust was in the air, but that wasn't unusual. We drank coffee as we gathered at Gloria's, and then set off for the river. Arriving there we women lugged bedrolls and supplies from where we parked to our launching place, while the men pumped up the two rafts. The Boquillas ranger, John Palmer, helped us get ourselves out in the river, saying we were foolish to go because of the wind, but we didn't want to give up. In our raft, Mildred and I on one side, Pat and Bob on the other, manned the oars. As we went around that slight bend before reaching the canyon, the rowing immediately became much harder, and when we were directly in front of the canyon the wind caught us, and even with the four of us using all our strength, it blew us back the way we had come. The white-capped waves splashed over the sides into the raft. We were helpless. When the wind died down for a minute, we pulled for the Mexican side (the only one we could get to) and held a consultation. The powerful wind rattled the dry cane around us like dead bones clacking.

We decided to wait for the wind to settle but time passed, everyone grew colder and colder, the wind kept pouring out of the canyon, and we knew we could make no headway. We re-boarded the rafts and tried to return to our launching place. But the current coming toward us, and the wind driving from behind us made a trap—the rafts couldn't go forward and couldn't go backward. They turned round and round in one spot, out of our control. When we finally brought both boats to the U.S. side, we stepped onto land with relief, leaving Pat and Stanley to struggle through the wild water, towing the rafts to the launching place. The rest of us hiked to the jeep, and Bob radioed for George to come help us get to the Boquillas ranger station where John Palmer had taken Stanley's car. Then we met Pat and Stanley at the landing and unloaded the rafts—quite a job, wet and cold as we were. Meanwhile Bob made a huge pot of coffee over a fire and two rocks, and by the time George came we were eating lunch. He couldn't help making a little fun of us despite our disappointment and our frozen and bedraggled condition. But he said the minute the wind changed after we had left Panther Junction, he knew we'd be fighting it, so he wasn't surprised at our call for help. A ranger from Carlsbad appeared from somewhere and helped with the deflating of the rafts and carried some of the stranded passengers to the Boquillas ranger station. We had coffee there again. Gloria's mother played Jean's piano, and we sang and danced.

You should see how they've fixed Jean's back porch—you remember how it overlooks the river. It now has a fireplace—very nice. I've liked that house since I first visited Pat and Mildred there. Did you ever notice that the ceilings are made of river canes? Topped with tar and cement, Pat said.

The group separated there, planning to meet at Panther Junction to claim our belongings. I went in George's car with Mildred, Gloria, and her mother. We detoured to look at the new water reservoir at the old Graham Ranch. I'd never been there before. It's being developed into a recreation unit, George said.

From there to the Giles' house and finally home again—weary and gritty, with the sand in the air growing thicker every minute. I learned a great deal today that will be of use when we go again. Also George showed us some interesting things along the way. You remember the day I was on the river with you and we got out and examined the cables of that ore trolley? I don't know why I've always thought it was florespar ore that had been hauled on it, but George said it was very rich silver ore from a mine in the Fronterisias. They used to haul it from the river in wagons, and he showed us an old wagon roadbed that had been cut out of the ground and the sides piled high with gravel and some dirt. At a distance we saw a cave where wild bees live. A crude ladder, two stories high but disjointed, led up to the cave. Aileen

MARCH 14, 1954 – SUNDAY - PANTHER JUNCTION - 9 P.M.

Dear Mama and Daddy,

Friday was such a hot, sultry, windy day here that I remarked to Gertrude if this were Alabama we could expect a tornado. In Big Bend it brought a different kind of weather change that affected our Boquillas Canyon trip. By eight yesterday morning we had the rubber rafts inflated and loaded and in the river. I was assigned to Pat's boat with Mildred, Bob the Castolon ranger, and Gloria

Giles' mother. Stanley was in charge of the other raft with Doris, Frank, and Gloria. The wind was blowing very cold, hard, and gritty. I wore your long-handles, Mama, the only one of the women who did, and argyle socks Art gave me (his aunt knitted for him). The others froze but I was comfortable. Lost my hat twice, but they rescued it both times. Frank lost his forever, and Pat's ranger hat blew off but he retrieved it.

As we rounded the bend to approach the canyon head, the wind poured out of the canyon with such force it brought our raft to a standstill even with four of us paddling. White-capped waves came out of the canyon to meet us and washed into the boats. We struggled for an hour and only reached the canyon entrance. We knew that once we got inside the canyon, a return would be impossible because of the ripples and the current, so when the wind lulled for a few moments we headed for the nearest shore (Mexico) and held a consultation. At first we agreed to wait and hope for a change in weather, but as we stood there the wind blew stronger and colder and grittier. The vote to try to return to our launching place was unanimous.

Once again in the boats for a reverse trip, we found ourselves caught between the current in front and the wind in back and could go neither way. Finally we had to get out on the nearest U.S. land and hike back to the landing while two of the men towed the rafts in the river. Fortunately, the jeep was still where we left it parked (someone was supposed to come for it because we never expected to return to it). Using the jeep radio, Bob called Panther Junction for George to come help us get home. First we unloaded the rafts and deflated them, and Bob built a fire and made coffee. When George showed up we were eating lunch. I came back in George's car. He took us by an old ranch place to see some work they've been doing on a recreational area, and I saw scenery I've never seen before. At Panther Junction the dust was so thick the mountains behind the school were completely invisible.

This morning Nealie came for me. At Government Springs we made two lemon pies and had delicious steak from the Gulliher ranch for dinner. Boots helped me study my Spanish lesson. The class laughs at me talking Spanish— I don't know what they would do if they didn't have Bo (Gertrude's husband) and me to laugh at—but he and I know what we're saying. Mae and Steve joined us at Government Springs for supper and after visiting a while they brought me home. The dust is still thick and the wind very cold.

I know my handwriting is terrible, but I didn't realize quite how terrible until Willie interpreted a recent grocery order of mine as requesting forty lemons. He thought there must be a mistake, but how could he risk it? He couldn't leave me without forty lemons if that was what I needed. He decided I must be planning to make lemonade for the whole school. From several sources he scrounged up forty lemons and left them in my kitchen the following Sunday morning. I've used most of them (the lemon pies at the Dotts' for instance) and will serve the Girl Scouts refreshments the last Wednesday of the month.

The latest word is we'll try Boquillas Canyon this coming weekend. AK

MARCH 21, 1954 - ALPINE - 10:15 A.M.

Dear Art,

This is the morning I was supposed to wake up in a sleeping bag at Marafa Vega in Boquillas Canyon. Instead, I am at the Alpine hotel and covered in calamine lotion. I was a sight to see but not so much a sight now. Thursday afternoon I broke out all over in an angry red rash. Friday I was worse. I'd never had an allergy before but what I had seemed like an allergy. Mae thought I was poisoned. Gertrude thought I had chicken pox. Mae brought me to the doctor Friday night. He gave me two shots and told me to stay in town through Sunday. He thinks a sore throat I had earlier in the week and nervous tension caused me to be sick, but I don't agree with him because I've had sorer throats and worked under greater pressure and this has never happened before. Anyway I went to see him twice yesterday; he gave me another medicine, and I'm on my way to see him for another shot as soon as I finish this.

It's been an enjoyable weekend even so. The doctor showed me the cocker spaniels and African basenji dogs he raises to sell. I had never seen any of the latter. They don't bark and are very cute. The cockers were leaping everywhere and barking every breath. They were adorable, especially the little ones. The doctor's sons take care of them.

I went to the Glenn Burgess camera shop, stayed several hours talking to both him and her. I learned a great deal about my camera and bought some accessories. He took me to lunch with his wife's blessing (she had to go somewhere else), and I saw three boxes of slides he had made on a Boquillas and backcountry trip in the park. The Burgesses, the Warnocks (he is biology professor at Sul Ross College), and another couple or two and Pete Koch are going through Boquillas Easter weekend. Glenn suggested I might go through with them as I missed my trip this weekend. That would be wonderful, with Pete to tell us everything about everything and Glenn to advise about picture making! I'd like that.

I checked out books from the public library yesterday for the children. I thought about that load of books you brought down to the school for me last year. Last night I visited with Mrs. Rogers, a most interesting elderly woman with a lovely home. She wants me to come stay with her this summer and go to school or just stay and do nothing. She needs companionship. The Burgesses and the Kochs are good friends of hers and she knew about me through them. But I can't—I have other plans.

I must end this. After I see the doctor, I'm to go to church and then to dinner with Mae's friend, and at four Roy Lassiter is to pick me up here with all my books, calamine lotion, other medicines, etc., to return to the park. Aileen

MARCH 23, 1954 - PANTHER JUNCTION - 6:30 P.M.

Dear Art,

This is ceramics class night, in thirty minutes. I've just finished collecting my tools—paring knife, wax paper, rolling pin—and now I'll take this little time to write you. We usually aren't finished with class until ten or later, and I'd like to bake cookies afterwards for the party Gertrude and I plan to give Jack and Millard Ray Friday afternoon.

Boots did get his transfer, and they are expected at Death Valley by April 5th. What will I do without them? Nealie was here last night almost crying. She wants to go because she recognizes the advantages. Boots will get a forty-cents-an-hour raise, and Jack can stay at home when he goes to high school, but she is sorry to leave her family and the people she has known all her life. I was certain they'd get the transfer (reasonably so, since Bob Mansell, who is already out there, was working for it), but I hoped it wouldn't happen until after I left Big Bend.

The weather has been mild, spring-like, and most amazing, moist! A few drops of rain fell during today. Everyone was excited, hoping for more and more. But not yet.

Today in school we saw *A Visit to Ireland* in color. The children were carried away with it. Beautiful! We thought we saw a leprechaun darting about in a clump of trees. I can't think of any place more different from Big Bend. We have so little greenery this spring you can imagine how they would enjoy Ireland. And those lakes and the wheat fields!

George is away now at fire school (Grand Canyon) and is leaving Easter for a trip into Mexico, and he just returned from a Mexico trip before he left for Grand Canyon. They are working hard for the international park.

In Girl Scouts tomorrow we are to learn the different knots. I'm afraid I've forgotten them so now I must practice tying. Aileen

MARCH 24, 1954 – WEDNESDAY - 9 P.M.

Dear Art,

Panther Junction is dark tonight, without power for the first time since REA came into the park last year. Grandma Larsen and I are probably the only ones in the settlement anyway, as there is a farewell party in the Basin for Boots and Nealie tonight. Inger asked me to go with them, but I begged off as Mrs. Bledsoe is to have a party for Nealie tomorrow night—a women's party—and I will go to that.

We are having the worst dust storm ever. The wind is even stronger than it was the weekend we tried to go through the canyon, and the dust is sifting into the house under the door and around the windows. Everyone has been coughing and sneezing today. This afternoon Inger told me that two small dogs in Marathon have died of dust pneumonia.

Grandma Larsen is leaving tomorrow; Lon is taking her to El Paso to catch the plane. I went across the arroyo after Scout meeting to say goodbye and take her a small jar of Indian chippings for her other grandchildren. We never did go on that walk to collect chippings for them as she wanted to do. I am most fond of her and will sure 'nuff miss her. That's too many gone out of my life at once with Boots, Nealie, and the boys going so soon.

Did you know Mrs. Larsen is Lutheran? I didn't until a week ago when she was here visiting me. She commented on the Bible on my table. She more than commented—we talked a long while about it. This afternoon when I left her house she followed me outside to give me a slip of paper on which she had written some Bible references. She said they were verses that had helped her a great deal and she hoped they would be helpful to me. She said, "Do not fear; He will take care of you." I know He will, but sometimes in the hurry of living I forget.

I was so pleased to see there was another letter from you in today's mail— I got one last mail day too! Had no time to read it before Scout meeting, but I did open it to make sure there was a letter in the envelope. All during the meeting while we tied knots and distributed lemonade and cookies and sang the National Anthem, I anticipated being alone so I could read it.

Now I have read it, and I am so sorry that your work is not going well there and that you feel discouraged. I know there are bad people wherever one is, but I do believe that most people are good, and I wish that you might find it so. My greatest discouragement concerns myself and how far short I fall of being the kind of person I'd like to be. What wisdom and understanding I need and don't have, through my own fault, I know.

I've been writing by the light of my flashlight, and now it's growing dim. That's the signal for closing. Please cheer up. Aileen

MARCH 25, 1954 - PANTHER JUNCTION

Dear Mary Alice and All,

You all have probably had plenty of Big Bend sand blowing over Alabama. Yesterday it was flying especially thick and fast. Everything was covered with dust this morning and everybody is sneezing and coughing.

I missed the Boquillas Canyon trip after all. They went last weekend, but I had to go into town to the doctor. Thursday afternoon I began breaking out and growing knots, like an allergy, and by Friday afternoon my hands and face were swollen and I was covered with welts and itched so I was miserable. Mae took me to Alpine to the doctor; then she went on to Odessa to see Ray as the doctor wanted me to stay in town for treatment.

He gave me shots and medicine and said nervous tension might be part of my problem.

It had been a hard week. Bill, Jess, and Joyce are so far behind my fifth graders, it's like teaching five grades now instead of the four I've been struggling with. They need help with every little thing, and skipping the fourth grade has certainly left them unprepared for upper grade work.

I am all right now and trying to take things a bit easier. Grandma Larsen left the park today to visit with some of her other children. I will miss her. Boots and Nealie are leaving Tuesday for their new place at Death Valley. I hate to see them go! We are all going to the ranch for one last time tomorrow afternoon. I made cookies this afternoon for a party Gertrude and I are giving for Jack and Millard Ray in school. AK

APRIL 1, 1954 - PANTHER JUNCTION

Dear Art,

This week we've been having days like we used to have when you were here—very warm, and long, peaceful twilights. Boots and Nealie left on Monday, in the afternoon. Eighteen children are left in school now.

Gertrude and I had the school party for Millard R. and Jack on Friday. By the time it was over the school was a shambles—drinks spilled on the floor, Boots' and Gertrude's cigarette ashes everywhere, coffee cups and crummy cookie plates scattered on the table. Before the children were out of sight Mr. Evans brought three officials to tour the school—one from Washington, the other two from Santa Fe. I tried to welcome them cordially, but I was as big a wreck as the school. Steve and I had to laugh after they were gone. I hope they don't think we run our school the way we run our parties.

Saturday the Dotts took steak and I two lemon pies and pear salad to the Gulliher ranch for what we thought would be a quiet farewell evening. But people came in droves from Marathon and all the ranches around. Oh, those piercing yells that explode from these West Texans periodically at parties, the unrelenting noise, the drinking, the swearing, and wild dancing! What beery odors and powerful-smelling after-shave lotions! The food was wonderful (most everybody had brought a dish), and I tried to creep away often to the kitchen and hide a while. West Texas in the raw, and it was three before I was in my bed at Panther Junction.

I planned to sleep late Sunday, but the grocer came at eight so I had to dress in a hurry. Boots came for me soon afterward, and I spent the day ironing and helping the Dotts get ready for the moving van. In the late afternoon we drove to the Basin for a very good supper with Bo and Gertrude. We came back to my place early and said our goodbyes. I'll never forget them.

Monday Art Minish came over to school with the camera accessories Glenn ordered for me and to tell me that Mae was very sick. They radioed the doctor to come to the park to see her. He came but wasn't sure what ailed her. He gave her medicine that seemed to help. Tuesday afternoon I rode over to the Basin with Gertrude and the children and was glad to find her much better. Doris and Frank invited Steve and me up to their house for supper (Stanley has gone to Grand Canyon for a load of dynamite). I never expected to eat at Doris's house! That's one of the nice things about this year though—her changed attitude toward me. She is always cordial now.

At Inger's ceramics class I made a panther, and I hope, hope, he doesn't explode when he's baked so you can see him. He's very pantherish-looking, and I want to keep him for a Big Bend souvenir.

I've been trying to make a picture of a roadrunner. One day in Green Gulch when we saw one Mae stopped the car and I sped after it with the camera but it vanished. I know they live around the school and must drink at my water pans but I don't see any. I hear them calling—sounds like two rocks being rubbed together rapidly. On hot days last year about noontime I could look out the window and see one coming for water. They are so homely and cute.

This morning for a few minutes the children and I watched a butcherbird on a bush outside the school window. I managed to make a picture of a Spanish dagger blossom before a deer ate it. Even the lecheguilla is dying now for lack of water. We need rain terribly.

I enjoyed the clippings you sent. We've been following the stories about the discovery of the Lewis and Clark papers because two of my groups have had Lewis and Clark in history. Aileen

Dear Art,

This is a very cozy late afternoon. The sky is gray and heavy; the thunder is rolling overhead, the lightning is auguring down, but far away, and the air smells wet. Rain is falling in any direction I look—even on the Chisos, though not right here at Panther Junction. Everybody is jubilant. Steve, Karen, and I were on my patio just now when Inger came running out of her house across the arroyo calling and pointing. The rain had just moved out of the Chisos and was falling between the school and my three mountains—Pummel, Wright, and Panther. The desert smells wonderful.

Yesterday was my birthday—33—the most alone birthday I ever spent. Panther Junction inhabitants were in town at the rodeo or else sleeping late and staying close.

Only two of my recent letters to you have been mailed from Alpine—the one Stanley mailed about the panther and the one I wrote you when I was in to see the doctor. All the others have been mailed from Hdqtrs., but sometimes when someone is going in to town, the Panther Jct. mail is sent with them instead of being sent over to the Basin to wait for the regular mail. That may explain the Alpine postmarks.

Friday night Mae, Ray, Steve, and I went on the river to fish. We turned off the Boquillas road and went in the direction you showed me you all went to fight a fire once. We found a lovely green valley where the park has set out willows, and there is a grove of old, large salt cedars. Steve and I walked up the river exploring, then while Ray and Mae fixed supper we went downriver looking at the many strange tracks in the mud. One set looked like a small dragon's footprints. The sun had set—way gone—when we came back. We could smell the campfire, and a wonderful wind was blowing in the salt cedars (tamarisks, Col. Raborg called them). So beautiful and perfect an evening! After supper (steaks, frijoles, and lemon pie with coffee) the moon was so bright Steve and I took another walk; the road made a square around the meadow with all that green grass, so we could explore it without a light—the moonlight was so strong, though we sometimes sank above our ankles in that soft, soft dust. Never such stars as these!

Steve came over the mountains this morning with Mac Waters to spend the day with me. After lunch we went to Garrisons' to complete our last week's ceramics lesson that was too long for one class period. Now he has been reading on the patio but it's dark and the lightning is closer so he's come inside. Mae is to pick him up tonight on her way in from Odessa.

Important Odds-and-Ends: I've heard that white skunks have been seen in the Basin, but I've seen only the regular black-and-white ones, and they are handsome enough. Mae is well now. Steve has had the cast off his wrist for two weeks. I spent last Sunday with Patty and Etta at Hot Springs.

The storm is roaring down on us now; the rain is increasing. I must fix some supper. Poor Mae might be stranded on the wrong side of Tornillo. Good night. Aileen

APRIL 11, 1954

Dear Mary Alice and All,

Yesterday was my birthday. I spent the day at home, working. In the afternoon an elderly man and his wife from Kent, Texas, came by to see the school. He is thinking of applying for it. They stayed quite a while and seemed to like it very much.

I ironed last night. Willie and George brought the groceries. Willie is going to stop bringing groceries the 24th of this month but another Marathon grocer is taking over.

We are having a wonderful rain now. On the ranches around the park I could see it raining yesterday and now on us today. Everybody is rejoicing. When I was to the Gullihers' with Boots and Nealie before they left, Fred and them were burning the spines off the cactuses for the animals. They said as soon as they cleaned a cactus ready for eating the sheep descended on it in a great bunch and gobbled it down. I know the Gullihers (and their sheep!) are happy tonight. One of the dishes I took to the ranch that last time was the pear salad you make, Mama, of pear halves filled with grated cheese and mayonnaise topped with a maraschino cherry. It was so pretty, and every bite was eaten. They said they had never had anything like that.

Steve spent the day with me. Mae expected to be back from Odessa to pick him up by six and it's now eight. I know the creeks will be up. I hope she's not stranded. Steve and I have now decided we'll have cornbread for supper with butter and milk so I must arise and fix it. AK

APRIL 13, 1954 - 8:15 P.M. - PANTHER JUNCTION

Dear Art,

I'm going to bed early tonight—most tired—but will write you a "note" beforehand. I've rearranged the room—the bed is down alongside the windows now so the last thing I see at night and the first thing in the morning is the sky. With the windows open, now that spring is here, it is wonderful.

Just after supper I took a walk toward the Chisos—sky gray, ground damp, cool enough for a coat. The ocatillos are beautiful back near Pummel, loaded with scarlet blossoms. The wild animal scent was everywhere because of the dampness. I found a choice Indian "blank." Had to come back because of the rain.

There is a great deal of news I've been forgetting to tell you: Pete has closed Hot Springs. Too great a drain financially, Etta said. The last Sunday I spent there was also Etta's last weekend there. The Dotts are enjoying Death Valley—a great deal of social activity (they had heard there was none) and a swimming pool, too. After school is out in May park personnel will move to the mountains to a place called Wildrose. Jack's class is to tour Hollywood and L.A. at the end of school. He is excited about that.

The Panther Junction Girl Scouts will end tomorrow for this year. We'll have a cookout at Irene's. She says she won't take them another year.

The other night after supper I sat out on the patio. The owls were hooing (not hooting) gently in the arroyo behind headquarters. One skunk comes to the patio now, and four different foxes that I recognize.

I hope you won't be disappointed to hear that I've dropped Spanish. I never had time to prepare for class—always there was something I needed to study for school. After preparing my other lessons my poor mind rebelled at struggling with Spanish.

This afternoon when I was walking I decided I must be mistaken about the roadrunner sounding like two rocks being rubbed together rapidly. The bird that makes that sound seems to be a dull brown one that flies low from bush to bush.

George came over yesterday to invite the school to a fire drill in the Basin Friday. We have a holiday that day so most of the children will go, but I think I won't.

Now a storm is coming from behind Panther Peak. Thunder and lightning. Goodnight. Aileen

APRIL 14, 1954 - 10:30 P.M.

Dear Art,

I'm back from ceramics class where I glazed the tile I had made, also a little bowl, and used a knife to make my panther smoother.

Saw George. He's just returned from the Keyes ranch in the Rosillos. The Keyes had planned to move out of the Big Bend with all of their animals because of the drouth. (I don't know if they'll stay after this rain or not). Mr. Keyes is going panther hunting tomorrow. George put in an order for a skin suitable for a rug for me. Not that I want a panther killed, but if it's going to be, why not use as much of its beautiful self as possible?

Since all the rain—Mrs. Bledsoe said a six-foot wall of water passed Lajitas—I thought perhaps the Burgess's canyon trip might be postponed but Lon was just in from town a while ago and said Glenn sent word to be ready by nine o'clock Saturday morning. We'll come back late Sunday. It's Mariscal Canyon, Art, and I'm delighted. It is the most beautiful of the three canyons, I've heard. I'm disappointed Pete can't go.

Some slides I had made came today. I wish you could see them: A deer in my yard (I stood on the patio and the deer stood between me and my two Spanish daggers); three little Mexican goatherds across the Rio Grande, with ocotilla in the foreground and ducks flying in the sky. (The river was full of ducks that day when I was last at Hot Springs with Etta). Also several of my pet fox. Pictures of him have to be time exposures, and they show movement but some of them are quite good. He never comes before night, not even now that darkness comes so late. At five o'clock this morning the milk bottle clanged on the porch; I got up to look and there he was. I wonder how long he had waited.

Col. Raborg is in the park. He came to school this afternoon while I was at the Girl Scout cookout at Irene's. He left word with Gertrude that he will be back. Liz is in North Carolina with a daughter who has just had a baby. I'm looking forward to seeing him.

It rained all last night, and we've just had another rain now. Tornillo Creek ran tremendously last night, we heard. Bill, Jess, and Joyce got stuck crossing it this morning. They had to push their car out. Good night. Aileen

APRIL 20, 1954 - PANTHER JUNCTION - 9:30 P.M.

Dear Art,

Our Easter trip through Mariscal was just about perfect. We had a most interesting group: Glenn and his son, Don; Mr. and Mrs. George Merrill, ranchers from the Davis Mtns; their son Martin who is just back from Korea; Chester and Jean Gleason, who made movies of the trip for television; Dr. Málaga, a Peruvian, and his Cuban wife; and Dr. Don Mason, from your own Minn., but now fresh from Montgomery, Alabama, where he is working with the health dept. The last three named are here on an international health commission, studying rabies in vampire bats. They have been exploring caves in Big Bend and in Mexico, collecting specimens.

Since all of us had special interests we agreed in the beginning to bear with one another. That is, when the bat people wanted to explore a cave, we were to patiently wait for them; when the movie man wanted shots we were to oblige him and not look at the camera; when Glenn, Martin, and I wanted to make pictures, they were to wait for us. And just about every time Glenn made a picture I made one too, and I took his advice about shutter speed and lens openings. I'm hoping for some good ones! I made about forty-two slides in all, and after my film ran out Glenn made several on his camera for me.

On Saturday morning I rode with the health commission people to the Solis ranch on the river road beyond San Vicente where we were to embark. Dr. Málaga told me he had met two men who were painting at Maggie's the day before. When we stopped at San Vicente I asked Maggie about them, thinking one might be Col. Raborg. Maggie said it was he, but she hadn't seen him that day. He had inquired about me, she said. She promised to tell him I would be back Monday, and we continued to the Solis ranch.

We left the bat people's car, Glenn's station wagon, and the rancher's pickup at the Drakes' house, and Mr. Drake took us and our belongings over a very rough road in his huge truck—it has fifteen gears and he has to change

Easter Morning at Mariscal Canyon. Photo by Glenn Burgess.

the oil only every thirty-thousand miles. I've a picture of it—it will run on gasoline or butane.

We ate lunch standing in the mud of the river, between taking turns pumping air in the boats. The river was so muddy it looked like a rich chocolate malted milk. (Before the trip was over I was so hot and thirsty I could almost have drunk it gladly.)

We had many rapids to go over even before entering the canyon. The bat people (I'm not being rude, but that's the simplest identification) ripped a hole in their raft to begin with (something we all feared doing), and we waited while they repaired it. How exciting those rapids were! The men did the paddling and we women were free to look and enjoy everything.

Just inside the canyon we parked on a rocky beach and made pictures while the bat people climbed the canyon wall to investigate three caves on the American side. I so regret not going with them! When they climbed down, Dr. Málaga said he had been in caves all over the world but the small one he had just explored was the most beautiful cave he had ever seen. The walls and ceiling were covered with green quartz crystals arranged in circular, wheel-like patterns, and the setting sun shining in at the cave mouth lighted them brilliantly.

Toward the end of the day we found an ideal place to camp—a beach near the water for the kitchen, and a higher, dry place for sleeping. Glenn expected high water during the night, as Presidio upstream had been flooded the day before. He wanted everything to be out of the way of the water.

Our raft couldn't land right away because we chased an oar one of the men dropped and went way down the river. We were battered by swift, rough water, monstrous rocks and snags, before catching the oar lodged against a boulder. (We feared the snags most because they could puncture our raft). Then we realized it was impossible to row our raft back to the camp. And the distance was too far and the way too rugged for us to carry our equipment. Glenn decided the only way we could go back was for one person to stay in the raft (being the smallest, I was chosen) and use the paddle to keep it off snags and boulders while Martin, on shore, towed it back to camp. The American side was too rough for him to tow from, so he climbed like a goat all over the boulders of the Mexican side pulling until he could go no farther. Then he got in the boat, helped me row to the American side where he got out again and continued pulling through some of the worst parts and got our boat (and me) safely back to camp. At first I was scared, the water was so swift and turbulent and so noisy I couldn't hear what they were hollering from shore, but when I saw I could handle it, I had a wonderful time. It was the most exciting part of the trip.

We had a delicious supper, the main dish being steak from the rancher's own critters. Sitting around the fire afterwards was one of the nicest parts. The sky was so beautiful way, way up there. And when the moon rose, we couldn't see it but we watched its light creep down the canyon wall toward us. We went late to our sleeping bags on the upper level. I didn't fall asleep for hours. The moonlight was too bright, the Rio Grande coffee too strong, the river too loud, and Dr. Málaga's snoring too unmusical, I guess. Anyway, I saw the moon when it came in view over the Mexican wall of the canyon. How beautiful it was, and how the river canes rattled in the wind. I found out next morning I wasn't the only one awake, but everybody was so still none of us suspected we weren't alone in our insomnia.

I did finally go to sleep though and was awakened next morning by the crows cawing over us. Then I heard the cañon wrens—what a sweet call and how it echoed against the canyon walls. The sky was blue and clear and the air wonderfully cool, a perfect Easter day. My watch said six-thirty.

Most of the morning we fooled around making pictures and talking. Everyone was so congenial and interesting. I especially enjoyed Don Burgess, who had a bird book (you have one like it: A Guide to Western Birds, by Peterson) and talked to me about the different birds around us. He showed me the Colima warbler in his book. When Steve and I go to the South Rim (maybe next weekend) I'm going to look for one. One of his interesting hobbies is collecting bird feathers. He's young but knows a great deal.

As we progressed deeper into the canyon the scenery became ever more beautiful. At one place the others waited while those of us with cameras went with Glenn way up on the side to make pictures looking down on the canyon. Very hot, but very worthwhile. We saw a black metal barrel on the Mexican side—a deserted wax camp, and I remembered when you and the other rangers went on that raid last year in Mariscal.

In the afternoon we came into parts of the canyon that were the most beautiful of all—huge, still pools of water reflecting the cathedral-like walls, great blue herons flying overhead. We saw a heron nest low on the canyon wall. At one place we saw a beaver, bright brown, before it slipped into the water. A bank beaver, they called it. The only other animals we saw were burros.

Toward the end we had to get out often and wade and pull the rafts after us. The Drakes had brought the Merrills' pickup to their pumping station and left it for us. We went to the Drakes' house and from there to Maggie's at San Vicente. By then dark was coming. The store was dim inside with only kerosene lamps burning and crowded with people drinking, smoking, and talking. And it was in that dimly lit crowd that I saw Col. Raborg for the first time. We were so pleased to see each other! We found a place on the porch where we could talk. He asked about you, of course, and sends you his regards.

And now today—we've had rain again, which is very good. Col. Raborg came as he had promised, but the rain was falling so hard he had to sit in the car a while before getting out. Once inside he recalled that last year when he and Liz were here a hard rain came while they were eating supper with you and me.

He looks well, and we had an enjoyable visit. He and a friend, Bill Bowers, are staying at Hot Springs, illegally, since no one is operating the place now. But that was where they had planned to work from, and they didn't want to change their plans after finding Pete had closed. Col. Raborg is heartbroken because the park has dynamited the bathhouse at Hot Springs. He showed me some of the sketches he's made since arriving in Big Bend this time, and some watercolors he's done, and I liked them very much. He's coming back next Monday afternoon to show me what he does this week.

Thanks for the article you sent about saving the panther. I read it to the children yesterday morning, and they enjoyed it. Bill and Jess, being ranch boys, can't see any sense in preserving the panther, but they listened with interest as I read.

Mae ate supper with me last night and spent the night. Steve and some of this year's fireguards went through Mariscal yesterday and today. I've heard no reports but I hope they had a wonderful time. Aileen

APRIL 25, 1954 - 8:40 P.M.

Dear Art,

Rain! Every night since Tuesday we've had terrific clouds with much lightning, thunder, and rain. And how the desert is blooming! About one o'clock this afternoon I went for a walk toward the Chisos with the camera. The sun was bright but the breeze was cool, and everything smelled so good! The pitayas and hedgehog cacti were beautiful. But later in the afternoon I went with Mae and Steve to Persimmon Gap where they are absolutely breathtaking. The hills out there look like rose gardens. We were glad to find the white pitaya cactus again this year but its blooms had closed because the sky was overcast and it was late. Picture-making was out of the question. Anyway I had only the tag end of the roll left—past zero.

At the gap we talked with Mildred for a while. She asked about you and said tell you "hello" for them. Their little girl is walking—she is so cute and fat. Her hair is very curly. She is much like Pat.

We went by Dagger Flat to see how things were there. Not a dagger blossom, apparently not a one bloomed this year. Many young dagger plants were dead. The other day a truck from Sul Ross reported at Persimmon Gap Ranger Station that they had permission to take up some of the giant daggers for the college. The truck proceeded to Dagger Flat while Pat radioed George and found out no one had given them permission. But before park officials could stop them, using the trucks and winches, they pulled up twenty of the giant daggers. The park allowed them to keep the twenty, but no more. One of the professors claimed the park superintendent had said the school could have them.

This past week I made pictures of a beautiful red racer, about four to five feet long (Bill and I say five feet; Steve and Jess say four feet) and about two and a half inches thick. On this particular day Gertrude had forgotten her lunch so I invited her to lunch with me. We were in my kitchen when Petra called me, saying the boys were killing a snake. Out I dashed, and found four of my boys, who were supposed to be in our room peacefully eating lunch, throwing boulders at this lovely rosy-red snake. It was seriously hurt before I got there, but I hoped it might recover. It's strange how the boys' sympathy went to the snake afterwards. Bill moved it in the shade, and the others worried about it, but the buzzards got it before long.

On Thursday night on the way to the Grapevine Hills with Mae and Steve, we found a run-over rattler near the Panther Junction turn-off. It was hardly damaged so we photographed it. Then Steve cut off its rattles—ten rattles and a button.

You wrote me that one night when you were here you saw a strange thing cross the road near Boots' house. That sounds very much like what happened to the Dotts and me as they were bringing me home one night. I intended writing you about it, but then we saw the panther on the Basin road, and I forgot it. Our incident happened like this: About 10:30 one night we were driving toward Panther Junction and had just passed the Basin turn-off. We were looking ahead. I saw much light reflected on the right side of the road, like those highway posts with reflectors, but I knew that was the wrong side of the road for a post. Just then Nealie leaned forward and said, "Is that a car taillight up there, or what?" and a shadow crossed the road in a most peculiar way. I can't describe the movement it made, but it was so different from anything we knew Boots zoomed with great speed to the place where It had crossed, and whirled crosswise of the road so the headlights shone in the direction It went. We saw nothing. But we all are convinced it was a panther. Or can it be the spirit of Alsate, and you saw him too?

Thursday night Mae, Steve, and I plan to go to Dugout to make pictures and eat after it's too late for pictures. On Friday I'm to spend the night with Mae, and Steve and I plan to hike to the South Rim.

I must say good night now. It is getting late. The wind is rising but there is no sign of a storm cloud. The lightning was most dreadful last night, and the thunder reverberated against the mountains and in the canyons. I was terribly frightened, but I was so glad you weren't in that tent across the arroyo or out on a mountain fighting fires. Aileen

APRIL 29, 1954 - SUNDAY - PANTHER JUNCTION

Dear Daddy,

Last Sunday when Mae, Steve, and I drove out of Dagger Flat we came suddenly upon a most strange animal crossing the road. It panicked, swerving and running along the road ahead of us, traveling at great speed and looking back once in a while. Unfortunately, the road dipped and curved and the animal was running into the sun, but all three of us had a concentrated look at it in the headlights and afterwards agreed it was as big as a medium-sized, powerfully built dog, bob-tailed, with a cat-like head and red-brown fur. A bobcat is what it looked like to us except for the color. Later when I described it to Jess and Bill, the ranch hands, they said it must have been a lynx. They've trapped many lynxes, red, yellow, and even blue ones. They consider them different from bobcats, but park people classify them as the same thing.

I'm enjoying ceramics class very much. Right now I'm making plates from a mold. I've made two already, though they've not been baked. I went by Inger's this afternoon to see the things she fired yesterday. One of my bowls was in the group, and it looked nicer than I could have imagined. Some of the pieces are skillfully made and beautiful. I'm eager to see how my panther turns out.

I pay eighty cents a dozen for eggs! The new grocery man started today. I was barely out of bed when he arrived at the crack of dawn. In putting away the groceries after he left I found he had forgotten to bring the six quarts of milk I ordered, the cottage cheese, and a loaf of bread. That means all next week without milk, but fortunately I have plenty of fruit juice; also a spare loaf of bread.

The park is certainly beautiful since the rains—breathtaking blossoms are everywhere. Some stalks that have been shriveled and ugly all year are now so gorgeous everybody runs for the camera.

The Garrisons and Shollys are back from their trip to Mexico. They were received at the governor's palace in Saltillo and were entertained by a congressman. AK

APRIL 29, 1954 - 9:50 P.M.

Dear Art,

Mae came up at lunch today to cancel our plans for picture taking at Dugout this afternoon and our South Rim trip. She suddenly decided to go to Odessa this weekend. I don't mind, much as I would like to go to the South Rim. This week I've felt so tired it is better that I stay home and rest.

This afternoon I went by Inger's to see some of our pottery she fired yesterday. It looks better than I imagined it could. Some of the pieces are beautiful. She hasn't fired the panther yet. I'm eager to see him finished. Right now we are working with models from plaster of Paris. I am making plates, while most of the others are making cups or ashtrays. Steve's ashtray that was fired yesterday is very good looking, and he has made two nice cups from his mold.

From Inger's I went to see Elizabeth Bledsoe to ask advice on graduating exercises for eighth graders. She helped me a great deal. Then I went by Reece's for a while and had a pleasant visit. The Basin ranger and his wife were there also. They are a nice couple with two children.

Then I came home and was cleaning the school when Col. Raborg and his friend, Bill Bowers, came with their sketches and watercolors, and Bill brought an oil painting of the del Carmens, from just below lower Hot Springs. It catches the beauty of those mountains more than any painting I've seen.

Col. Raborg had some well-done watercolors. I'd like to have a couple of them for my own! The best watercolor Bill had done—a pleasing desert scene—he intended sending to *Ford Times* with an article on Big Bend until I told him about Josef Muench's article and paintings last year. Bill is illustrating a guide-book to Mexico that a friend of his is writing. He and Col. Raborg seem to know Mexico intimately. One of Bill's paintings sold for $175, Col. R. said.

They talked most interestingly. You would have enjoyed them. Tomorrow or next day they are leaving the park. Col. Raborg said for us to be sure and keep in touch with him. In the fall he plans to go east for Liz, who is in Washington now, and he said he'd like to see us if we are there. He asked me to send you his regards, which I do so now.

The Shollys and Garrisons came back last Monday afternoon from their trip to Saltillo, Torreon, and Chihuahua City. Karen came over Monday night and told me about it. Most interesting. I don't know how much response they had for the international park, but they seemed to have been successful other-wise. Karen brought me a silver-and-onyx bracelet from Saltillo to match the earrings she bought me in Juarez when they took Mrs. Larsen to the plane in El Paso. Both pieces of jewelry match the pin from Taxco she gave me Christmas. All together they make a handsome set and good souvenirs of Mexico.

Tomorrow is Friday—mail day! Aileen

MAY 2, 1954 - PANTHER JUNCTION - 9:25 P.M.

Dear Art,

It's winter again tonight. A cool brisk wind is blowing quite a bit of dust through Big Bend.

Everyone in the park is saddened because Mr. French died suddenly yesterday afternoon while he and Mrs. French were driving to Alpine. The funeral is to be at three tomorrow in Alpine. I'm to keep the children here at school until the parents come to claim them. I don't mind. I feel I can make a better contribution in that way than if I attended the funeral.

This weekend has been busy in a quiet way. Friday night I did the weekly wash and packed some winter clothes to mail home. Yesterday I cleaned the school thoroughly, graded all my papers, and looked over the lessons for next week. In the afternoon I wrote letters and made two sets of cookies. I planned to send a box of cookies over to the office since they have treated me to coffee several times lately, but in this one twenty-four-hour period every cookie has disappeared except the ones I put away for the office, and I doubt if they will survive.

Bo and Gertrude came as I was taking the last pan out of the oven, bringing my milk that Mike forgot. They had tea and cookies, while telling me the news from town. They left by ten, and I was in bed soon after. I arose late this morning though—no Willie to get up for. (Mike did very well his first trip delivering. Everyone seems satisfied.)

Today I made several pictures of plants—Irene's ratama tree or paloverde which is in bloom; the prickly pear by the Big Bend mailbox; a low, lavender fuzzy plant I don't know; and two cactus plants up on Lone Mtn., where I went hiking with Danny this afternoon. (We were hoping for javelina but found only cactus, and not much of that.)

This was a hazardous day for Danny. We had a wreck on his bicycle. I was pulling him and hit a rock and down we crashed. We were able to get up, and the bicycle was able to run again, and Danny was willing to trust me again, but I wouldn't try it again. When we parked the bike at his house he startled a cottontail out of a bush, and I made its picture, a speedy blur, on their lawn. Remember that delightful evening when you and I and the Lundberg children watched the cottontails playing?

Then Danny and I undertook a project even more dangerous than riding a bicycle double on a Big Bend trail—we hiked to the very top of Lone Mtn by way of its backbone! You remember how wide-ranging the view is from up there—we were sure we could see all the way to the Grapevine Hills, and Marathon, and Hot Springs. All went well until we started back, straight down a sheer side. Danny slipped and fell a long way, bouncing from boulder to boulder and ending up in a catclaw bush. He did a great deal of groaning, but I was in a place I couldn't get out of at the moment. By the time I reached him he was on his feet plucking briars out of himself. Before we reached bottom, though, he was so tired he said his legs were coming apart. He wished for a helicopter, then he wished a buzzard would take him on its wing or that the wind would pick him up and set him down in his yard (which we could see from our mtn.). I worried he might not make it home, but we did, by a quarter of six.

The TV movie man is coming to school Wednesday to photograph the children inside the building and on the playground. He hopes to make pictures of some of my foxes too.

I've been wondering what we could do for the children the last day of school as a treat. I've decided, since they've been begging to see my slides, that I'll have a slide show. If Glenn still has that $18 projector I'll ask him to send it down. The children are in many of my pictures, especially at Lajitas, so they should enjoy seeing them.

I had coffee with the Gileses and George at noon after making pictures in the Panther Junction neighborhood. George said as far as he knew, and he subscribes to the *Ford Times*, Josef Muench's article about Big Bend has never appeared. Gloria lent me her April 5th *Life* magazine with the desert article you wrote me about. I enjoyed it very much. I was reading it when the Minishes came, and there is where some more of the cookies disappeared. We had an enjoyable visit.

The fox has come and eaten his supper of a luscious bone and some meat trimmings. Thank you for the informative sheet on hawks. When my students finish with it I'll send it to Mama as she is interested in hawks. Good night. Aileen

MAY 4, 1954 - PANTHER JUNCTION - 9:50 P.M.

Dear Art,

I'm just back from the children's dance program in the Basin. I went with the Shollys and Willie and Rene. The program was very cute. The costumes were almost works of art (that's with a little "a") and the children were good.

All the girls looked so pretty, especially Patty Koch with her dark hair and twinkling eyes (usually so solemn). Pete sat a while with me tonight, but just as he was going to tell me what he's been doing since he closed Hot Springs the loudspeaker went bad and he had to go fix it. I was sorry to miss what he had to say.

The Subletts asked those in our car and the Evanses and Garrisons to their house for coffee and delicious cake—yum. As we came down the mountain through Green Gulch I strained my eyes for a lion but no luck. But before leaving the Basin we saw a beautiful new moon framed by the Window.

It's sad to see all the dead shrubs and trees in Green Gulch—more dead ones than live ones.

Yesterday Gertrude went in town to Mr. French's funeral, and I had all the students all day. She came by just long enough to give me a schedule. That meant that I spent most of the day with her children, for they need help every minute. My children were so good though—they worked right on, with no foolishness. They behaved so well that when the day was over I served them the office cookies. They deserved them.

On the floor in my apartment one night I found a large critter that I thought at first was a scorpion, but after I squished it I found it was a mean-looking something I had never seen before. Bill and Jess say it is a vinegareete (spelling is doubtful but that's the way they say it). It isn't a vinegaroon, but the boys say it is poisonous like the vinegaroon.

Your account of the Mariscal wax raid sounded even more cold-blooded in your letter than when you told me about it last year. Poor burros. Poor Mexicans. Aileen

MAY 10, 1954 - PANTHER JUNCTION

Dear Art,

I'm lying on the couch, tired and sore from yesterday's adventure. Steve and I got up at 5:30 A.M., fixed our breakfast and packed our lunches. I intended taking a peanut butter sandwich but he said that you said that would never do on a hike, so I took a peach jam one instead. We were off by 6:30, though the sky was cloudy and we were hesitant at first because the main purpose of the trip was to make pictures.

On the trail to Concessions Steve discovered he was wearing the wrong shoes. He went back for his boots while I waited on the trail. At Juniper Flat fine rain began falling and for a time it looked as if we might get a soaking. A noisy group ahead of us, but out of sight, shouted, kicked rocks, and galloped up the trail and was soon out of hearing. Steve and I meandered along investigating anything that looked interesting. We found several lovely pitayas with the orange-red blossom—they don't grow below the mountains and someone said they don't grow outside the Chisos. I'm not sure about that.

I thought The Boot was spectacular, and also Boot Canyon was beautiful with what seemed to be red oak trees just growing new leaves. I hope they show up well in the picture. I looked for a quaking aspen but couldn't see anything as strange looking as it must be.

Before we got to Boot Spring we met some of the first party galloping back. We made way for them to pass, and good riddance! We thought we had the trail to ourselves now. We looked forward to eating lunch at the cabin, but when we arrived there the porch was filled with more of the first bunch lounging about. They were cordial, but I wanted to push on. Steve, however, made himself at home on the porch in the shade. I was standing by the steps undecided when one of the group stood up and spoke my name. It was Martin from the Mariscal Canyon trip! He was with Dr. Warnock and sixteen others from Dr. W's college ecology class. (I wondered how much plant life they had observed as they raced up and down the mtn.)

Martin and I compared notes on our Mariscal pictures, and he says Glenn Burgess will have a story about the canyon trip in the *Ft. Worth Star-Telegram.* He also told us something about the Rim trail even Steve didn't know and this was his ninth trip up. Do you remember where the two signs are near the Rim—one sign says "South Rim" and the other "Basin"? Martin said to the right of those two signs is an Indian mound. He showed us a most interesting Indian bead he had found on it, almost triangular with rounded corners, about the size of a half-dollar, and made of soapstone, he said. It was perfect except for a fragment missing from one corner.

We parted ways there, Steve and I going up, their group going down. Beyond Boot Spring the sight of a handsome gray squirrel made up our minds to eat lunch on the trail there, hoping it would pose for us. (It didn't.) While we were eating the rest of the college group dashed by going down. Martin had told us they hadn't seen any wildlife—no wonder. They even frightened us with all the noise they made. I'll complain to you about their other bad habits, if you will excuse me. They left debris along the trail, and they cut down century plants! We saw a total of ten freshly cut stalks. We took one that they had thrown in the trail to the shade for dissecting—to see how it was made inside. It was very juicy and tasted appetizing.

There are truly thousands of century plants along the trail in every stage of growth, and every stage is beautiful. I'm trying to make a picture record of each step in its development. The only one I haven't yet made is a plant in full bloom.

We found the Indian mound without difficulty and dug about in it (we committed a crime, too, didn't we?) but found nothing. The soil was very black, and the stones gave the impression of having been burned. We found three chippings nearby. I wanted to take a picture of the mound for you in case you hadn't seen it but by that time I had only two films left and I decided I'd better save them for the Rim.

I was glad I did. The South Rim literally took my breath away it was so beautiful and vast. I made one view looking east and one looking west and that was the end of the roll. Not a single extra slide did Mr. Kodak give me that time.

We heard so many wonderfully sweet birdcalls on the trail. What swift birds at the Rim—black and white, shaped like a swallow, and they whizzed by our heads at great speed. I forgot to look for the Colima warbler Don Burgess showed me in his book when we were in Mariscal Canyon.

On the way back I drank my last water at Boot Spring (the spring was dry). Steve had refilled his canteen from a pool in the rocks, and we had that but I didn't need any more until we descended into the Basin at 6:15 P.M. Mae had a delicious supper ready for us and we were ready for it.

This morning at the top of the mtn where the trail starts going down into Boot Canyon, Steve and I paused to eat an orange. While we sat there in the sun looking at the beautiful sky, and Nine Point Mesa and Corozon Peak in the distance, and listening to the birds, I said, "I wish Art were here." Steve said, "I wish so too." You should have been!

Aileen

MAY 11, 1954 - PANTHER JUNCTION

Dear Mary Alice,

The weather turned cold here last week. I had to hunt for a sweater. I am glad to know that you all are considering coming for me when school is out. I have a real plum to dangle in front of you—a special and cordial invitation to a ranch in the beautiful Davis Mtns, a real ranch, a working ranch. Some of the nicest people I've ever met, the Merrills, who were in the Mariscal group, want all of us to come. They invited us at the end of the canyon trip, and then Sunday when Steve and I were on our way to the South Rim (about fifteen miles round trip) we met Martin Merrill at the Boot Spring cabin. His folks had told him to be sure to reissue the invitation. They are all very nice and we would have a time we'd never forget. You could arrive on the 28th or shortly there-after. We are planning a simple graduation exercise on May 27th at night.

At one of our get-togethers, Rene, Willie's wife, told me about an interesting opportunity. She said she hadn't spoken to me about it before I handed in my res-ignation because she didn't want to take me away from the Big Bend school, but now she felt free to tell me that a wealthy ranching family asked her to approach me about becoming the governess for their two daughters. They own a beautiful ranch of thousands of acres, travel a great deal, fly their own plane, would treat me like a member of the family, and pay much more than I earn now. Would I be interested? It sounded like a storybook offer, but I told her I couldn't consider it.

I've just come from ceramics class. You all should see my panther. I think you'll like him. I've made three plates, a thing with a lid that's too big for a sugar dish but too small for a cookie jar (which is what it looks like), a bulb bowl, a tile for hot dishes, and I have one more piece to make.

I stayed last weekend with Mae (except for going to the South Rim with Steve from 6:30 A.M. to 6:15 P.M. on Sunday) and certainly enjoyed it. She gave me a permanent and I like it. AK

MAY 16, 1954

Dear Art,

Big Bend was never like this last year when you were here—it's raining again, and our last rain was only Friday night. This spring has been cool with only one or two hot days. But no giant daggers. Do you remember the beautiful cholla at the windmill road? You and I looked at it last year at two o'clock in the morning, well-chaperoned by Steve. Well, it isn't pretty this year, just ragged.

This has been a day of work for me since getting up about 8:30 to do my weekly wash. This afternoon I went to Inger's and glazed two plates. She will fire them next week along with the panther and another contraption I made. Next Thursday night the Garrisons are giving a barbecue to show off our ceramic masterpieces (and some of them really are masterpieces).

Next Wednesday we are giving achievement tests. I'm eager to see how the children rate but shrink a little from the testing for fear they won't do well. I may give the seventh and eighth grades their tests on Tuesday. Then a week from Thursday is the eighth grade graduation. Judge McGaughy or Peyton Cain (superintendent of Alpine schools) will probably be the speaker (the board is doing the inviting) and Laurie, pres. of bd., will award the diplomas.

Friday afternoon I took the long-delayed cookies over to the office and we had coffee. George was away but all the others were there. Lon and I were the last ones to leave the coffee room (he had shown me Freeman Tilden's book on Nat'l Parks, and asked if I wanted to buy a dollar copy for fifty cents. I said no, not because I'm not interested, but I thought you might have one, or maybe we can get one later with photographs.) Anyway, he said how grateful he and Inger are for all I've done for Karen, and there were tears in his eyes as he talked. But, as I told him, I can't take the credit for the really remarkable change in her since Christmas—her impudence and antagonism are gone, and she has worked quite hard. Apparently she made up her mind to change herself, and she has. I'm most glad for Lon and Inger's sake. They are two wonderful people, I think, and I've wished I could do more for them through Karen.

My dear Eligio. I wish I could know what will happen to him. He is so thin and so anxious of the other children's approval. And Petra . . . and all of them. The only three I don't worry about are Patty, Frank, and Karen. I know they will have every chance possible. But my others—some of them will probably end up in a shooting such as the one at Lajitas last Sunday. Petra, Eligio, and their family were right in the middle of it, but this time none of them was hurt.

I'm not feeling very cheerful this night. That's apparent, I expect. So many sad things have happened in Big Bend recently. I realize more than ever how far apart you and I are and how mortal we are.

The dogwood blossom and leaf you sent were beautiful, thank you. You did pick a perfect blossom. Don't you know the children here would enjoy seeing the dogwood trees blooming?

Yesterday I went to Alpine with the clerk and his family—the Arnolds. They are very pleasant but detest Big Bend. I visited the Mexican consulate. They gave me some colorful travel posters. I lunched with the Burgesses at that place I've been to with you across from the college. I added some of Glenn's slides to my Mariscal collection (the ones he made for me after I used all my film), and he is getting me duplicates of two of his. He let me have a duplicate of that slide the tourist made last summer of the lion sitting in the road near Panther Junction. How irritated I am with the lions. For two years I've searched for them to make pictures, and not a whisker have I seen. And here this tourist drives into the park and finds one sitting in the road in broad daylight almost in my front yard.

We took the library books back I had used here at school. You returned them for me last year.

Mae's friend from Alpine came to the park in the afternoon, the one I lunched with when I was sick with that allergy. We took her and her husband to Dugout for supper. Most beautiful there this time of year as you well know. The moon was nearly full, and the wind blew through the cottonwoods. That willow tree by the windmill is blooming, and the doves were calling when we first got there just after sunset. Never such stars as these Big Bend stars! How wonderfully lovely they were.

The Cliftons are now living near Marshall, Texas. They want me to visit them before I leave Texas, but I don't know. I'm very tired and ready to go home.

I'm enclosing Col. Raborg's note. As soon as I found out Muench's Big Bend pictures hadn't been published in *Ford Times* I notified him because his friend Bill had a beautiful watercolor of the Hot Springs area he wanted to send to *F.T.*, but he hesitated because he thought the other had been published. The "party" he mentions was coffee and cookies they had with me the last time they came. They had been out of coffee for about a week, I remember, so mine tasted especially good to them. Goodnight—Aileen

Dear Art,

Lon and Inger's barbecue is just over and it was wonderful—hundreds of people, from everywhere and an endless amount of delicious food. We had barbecued chicken, potatoes, green salad, that hot chile molé, pickles, frijoles, hot buttered bread, coffee, lemonade, cookies, and everything. After supper George showed a film that you would have enjoyed, *In the Beginning*. It is brand new. Lon said this is probably its first showing, and it is based on a talk given by a naturalist at Grand Canyon. Lon was instrumental in getting the picture made. It is in Technicolor and most beautiful—about the different ages of the earth as shown in Grand Canyon.

The ceramics we've made were on display inside and they looked well done. One thing I made and saw tonight for the first time since I glazed it wasn't thoroughly coated with glaze, though it's right cute. An enjoyable time was had by all!

Today I gave the seventh and eighth grades their achievement tests. I was well pleased with the results of the fifth grade test the other day, especially Patty and Eligio. Eligio averaged exactly where he is supposed to and Patty was above grade level. These tests today, as far as I checked, seem all right.

I've had no definite word from home that they are coming for me so earlier this week I wrote for a reservation on the night train from Alpine (Sunset Limited) but it will have to be Saturday night, much as I would like to leave Friday night. I'll have to clean the school and make a six weeks report and an annual report and so much else I can't possibly get away by Friday night. Stanley is to take my trunk in Thursday. Will I look foolish if I take the flowerpot containing my Pine Canyon plant in my hand on the train? I can't leave it behind. It's so handsome, and there is no way to pack it. You must see it.

I've just fed my foxes. Wonder what they will do when I'm gone. The quail stay on my patio from the time before I get up until sunset eating crumbs. One day last week I made a picture of the lame fox drinking milk out of the pan, but the day was late and gray so it may not be good. Steve has a good slide of a collared lizard.

It is thundering now. Every night we've had rain, much lightning and thunder, and last night much powerful wind. I worked out in the schoolroom on geography workbooks, and I thought this building would blow away. All the bad weather came from the southwest.

I have to write a note home, order some flowers for next Thursday night (for Frank and Karen, the graduates), a note to the Cliftons refusing their invitation, and a note to the Merrills. I had received two verbal invitations to visit Merrills at their Davis Mtn. ranch. On Wednesday came a written invitation; they said they would come to Alpine for me. They are all of them wonderfully nice, and I would have gone for a day or two if you hadn't told me you were coming to Alabama as soon as I arrive there.

I value the enclosed note from Pete and Etta. They sent me nineteen beautiful slides—you know what a master photographer he is. Wasn't that kind? Goodnight. AK

MAY 23, 1954

Dear Jane,

Today I finished packing—five boxes to mail, three to send along with the trunk. Only enough clothes hanging in the closet to see me through the week. I thought at first I couldn't be ready to leave until Saturday night but I have my plans made now so that I think I can go in Friday for the 7:35 Sunset Limited. I should hear from my reservation tomorrow as the Garrisons took my letter in yesterday. If I leave Friday—as I'm pretty certain I will—I'll get to Tuscaloosa about 5:00 A.M. That's too unearthly an hour for anyone to meet me, so I won't mind waiting.

The only thing I haven't found a place to pack is my cowboy boots. I surely can't leave them, but there is no place to squeeze them in. Even the two blankets are packed, so the only cover I have is the bedspread. If the weather turns cool as it has off and on, I'll turn to an icicle.

The achievement tests I gave this past week turned out very well. All the grades except the eighth have finished their textbooks. I hope to get the eighth through theirs this next week and get them safely graduated.

See you all soon—a week from today in fact. Aileen

MAY 23, 1954 - NIGHTTIME - PANTHER JUNCTION

Dear Art,

Only a note and it really must be a note, as it is ten o'clock. All day yesterday and today I've been packing. The trunk is ready for Stanley to pick up, and boxes of rocks, etc, are tied up all over the room—eight in all, some to go in the mail and some for Stanley to take. Only the cowboy boots Karen gave me aren't packed. I can't find any place to put them but I must bring them for a souvenir.

The Southern Pacific agent is trying to get a reservation for me on the Sunset Limited for next Friday night. I've begun work on my reports already, and I know the children who have to stay late at school for their ride home will help me clean the school so I should be ready to go with Roy at 4:30. I hope so! I am ready—plumb ready.

The achievement tests are all finished and charted. They turned out very well. Except Petra's didn't give a true picture of her intelligence—she was below her grade level in average even though she does excellent work in school. But it's the understanding of the English that handicaps her. In daily work I can explain meanings of terms to her, but this test certainly stopped her. I hope she never sees the results. She would be too disappointed. She sets high standards for herself and lives up to them. Aileen

MAY 29, 1954 - SATURDAY - 5 P.M. - NEW ORLEANS

Dear Art,

I've so much to tell you. I last wrote you in Wednesday's mail, I believe. On Thursday night we had our graduation exercise. Laurie brought us a roll of wire about seven feet high, which we stretched across the width of our room in front of my apt. door. We curved it slightly to make a background for a stage. Then we stripped most of Big Bend's trees for greenery to weave in and out of the open places in the wire. In the center of the wall of greenery we cut an archway and outlined it with flowers so that we had an attractive background for our program. The audience sat in Gertrude's schoolroom facing the stage. First the children danced three folk dances, then we closed the curtains that are normally between mine and Gertrude's room, so the "dignitaries" could arrange themselves on the stage: Mr. Lawson, the Methodist minister from Alpine, on the right of the stage, Peyton Cain beside him, Judge McGaughy, Frank, Karen, Laurie, Byram Waller (the new board member since Nealie left), Helen Minish, and me. (I've a program somewhere I've saved for you).

The children sang the invocation, Mr. Cain made his speech, Laurie (as president of the board) presented the diplomas, and I was poised to rise and introduce the minister so he could pronounce the benediction, but Laurie didn't sit down. He called Inger, and she came to the stage with two packages—gifts for me from my school parents and Girl Scout parents. I was really speechless. Usually they give gifts when people depart, I knew that, but there had been absolutely no evidence that I would get one. It took me a while to collect myself. We did get the benediction pronounced, and I opened the gifts—just what I needed! A leather case for carrying the camera and all accessories, even flash bulbs, and a file for slides. They are very very nice. Inger said they had had no idea what to choose until they asked Glenn Burgess. On the Mariscal trip I carried all camera accessories in a red bandana tied to my belt and thought nothing of it, but Glenn told them if I had fallen in the river all spare film, etc. would have been ruined. So he advised they buy the camera bag, and with the money left they bought the slide file. (My slides were in a box in the floor of my apartment. I was glad to have a better place to keep them.)

For Frank and Karen I ordered corsages—Stanley brought them down Thursday afternoon. For Frank the shop sent a red carnation, but for Karen they sent little orchids, beautifully arranged. I wish they had been more equal! Both eighth graders looked nice for their graduation and did their parts well. I guess there had to be one last example of the spirit of the Chisos at work— Reece arrived with a beautiful corsage she had made for Gertrude. As she pinned it on, she said, "I heard that Aileen had ordered corsages for herself, Karen, and Frank, and I wasn't going to have you be the only one without flowers." So it turned out that I was the only one not wearing flowers, but I didn't mind. I did feel a bit wounded that Reece thought I could be so careless of Gertrude's feelings. I only wish the shop had made Frank's flower more elaborate.

Glenn came also and made pictures. He is to send me a print of each he made.

Graduation night, May 27, 1954. Photo by Glenn Burgess.

Most of the goodbyes were said that night. Everyone was complimentary. Afterwards some of us went to Garrisons' for lemonade and cookies—Stan, Doris, Frank, and all the guests from Alpine. Finally to bed and up next morning early. We cleaned the school of the program debris, Helen came and showed the slides, and about eleven everybody went home. Gertrude and I worked on reports. Rather, I worked on reports—she had nothing done on hers. I had to do them both because then I had to make another report that summarized the year for both rooms. At times I was almost tearing out my hair. Inger had me to lunch—what a pleasant interlude, and the food was delicious! Afterwards I worked on the reports again. Karen cleaned the two bathrooms for me (how grateful I was!) and finally about 2:15 I cleaned the main part of the school (I thought about you doing it for me last year) and did the last-minute packing and cleaned my apartment. I was just going for the mail when Roy came for my luggage. I never dreamed I would have so much. I was delighted to see your two letters in the mail, and Roy excused me to read them while we drove out of the park. I was too occupied to take a last look at the Chisos!

In Marathon Roy and I stopped at Willie's drugstore to refresh ourselves. Rene fixed me a delicious chocolate malted milk. Roy and I reached Alpine at 7:15 P.M. The train was due at 7:35 but was about fifteen minutes late. The drugstore people were wonderful. They wrapped a big package of "stuff" for me that I hadn't had a box big enough for and are sending it and two other boxes by express for me.

I carried the Pine Canyon plant in a box. At this moment it is safely stowed in a locker but somehow one of its petals has been damaged and is shrinking.

The Merrills and Burgesses came to see me off and were a great help. You asked me to get a Pullman seat. I had intended to, as I knew I'd be very tired, but the Limited has only roomettes, drawing rooms, etc., besides coach seats. The roomettes were only about $8 more than a lower berth on the slow train so I took a fling and had one reserved. I was glad—it was so comfortable, besides all the fascinating gadgets. I slept from last night until past twelve today. Lunch was the only meal I ate on the train.

Do you know the Virginia warbler? The bird book says the Colima warbler is very similar to it.   Aileen

In December 1954 I married the ranger, Art Henderson, who by this time was stationed in Asheville, North Carolina, on the Blue Ridge Parkway. Later we wintered at Soco Gap above Maggie Valley, then were transferred to Washington, D.C., where Art realized his ambition of becoming a naturalist and where our daughter, Anne, was born. From the heart of Washington we moved to the beautiful but desolate Badlands of North Dakota (Theodore Roosevelt National Memorial Park at that time). After two years as naturalist-historian there my husband resigned from the National Park Service, and we lived in various places before returning to my childhood home in Alabama where we live today.

Aileen and Art Henderson now live in her family home in Brookwood, Alabama. Arthur Henderson is a retired naturalist historian who spent several years with the National Park Service. Aileen Kilgore Henderson is the author of *Treasure of Panther Peak*, a juvenile adventure novel set in Big Bend National Park.